simply graphic

clean & crisp design for scrapbook pages

spunky

Lexi

19 months

sweetheart

little model

From the Editors of Memory Makers Books

MEMORY MAKERS BOOKS

Denver, Colorado

Managing Editor MaryJo Regier

Art Director Nick Nyffeler

Contributing Editor Lydia Rueger

Photographer Ken Trujillo

Art Acquisitions Editor Janetta Abucejo Wieneke

Craft Editor Jodi Amidei

Graphic Designers Jordan Kinney, Robin Rozum

Production Coordinator Matthew Wagner

Administrative Assistant Karen Cain

Editorial Support Amy Glander, Emily Curry Hitchingham

Contributing Photographers Camillo DiLizia, Jennifer Reeves

Copy Editor Dena Twinem

Contributing Memory Makers Masters Amber Baley, Joanna Bolick, Susan Cyrus, Kelly Goree, Valerie Salmon, Jessica Sprague, Lisa VanderVeen

Memory Makers® *Simply Graphic*
Copyright © 2006 Memory Makers Books
All rights reserved.

Published by Memory Makers Books, an imprint of F+W Publications, Inc.
12365 Huron Street, Suite 500, Denver, CO 80234
Phone (800) 254-9124

First edition. Printed in the United States.
10 09 08 07 06 5 4 3 2 1

Library of Congress Cataloging-in-Publication Data

Simply graphic : clean & crisp design for scrapbook pages / [editor, Lydia Rueger ... et al.].-- 1st ed.
    p. cm.
  Includes index.
  ISBN-13: 978-1-892127-78-5
  ISBN-10: 1-892127-78-4
  1. Photograph albums. 2. Photographs--Conservation and restoration. 3. Scrapbooks.
  I. Rueger, Lydia.

TR465.S564 2006
745.593--dc22

2005058442

Distributed to trade and art markets by
F+W Publications, Inc.
4700 East Galbraith Road, Cincinnati, OH 45236
Phone (800) 289-0963

Distributed in Canada by
Fraser Direct
100 Armstrong Avenue
Georgetown, ON, Canada L7G 5S4
Tel: (905) 877-4411

Distributed in the U.K. and Europe by
David & Charles
Brunel House, Newton Abbot,
Devon, TQ12 4PU, England
Tel: (+44) 1626 323200, Fax: (+44) 1626 323319
E-mail: mail@davidandcharles.co.uk

Distributed in Australia by
Capricorn Link
P.O. Box 704, S. Windsor NSW, 2756 Australia
Tel: (02) 4577-3555

Memory Makers Books is the home of *Memory Makers*, the scrapbook magazine dedicated to educating and inspiring scrapbookers. To subscribe, or for more information, call (800) 366-6465.
Visit us on the Internet at www.memorymakersmagazine.com

IF

If I could know your thoughts
If I could know your dreams
If I could know your feelings
If I could know your likes
If I could know your troubles
If I could know your triumphs
Then I will know you!

-Mom-

Table of Contents

INTRODUCTION 6

concept

PAGES 8-35

Often it's the idea behind a page that makes others stop and take notice. See how artists made their pages more memorable by putting different spins on a variety of popular page topics.

type

PAGES 36-65

On graphic-style pages, titles and journaling often become important design elements. Learn to use appropriate font styles, positioning and more to support and enhance your designs.

image

layout

PAGES 66-95

Careful selection of page images, whether using a single photo or a group of shapes, can make your pages pop. Gather inspiration from artists who used images in a variety of ways to create impact.

PAGES 96-123

Striking concept, type and images come together on artfully arranged pages. Discover how a strong layout can help all page elements work together in ways that push them one step beyond the rest.

ADDITIONAL INSTRUCTIONS & CREDITS 124
SOURCES 125
INDEX 127

Introduction

Take a deep breath. Now imagine: clean lines…open space…simple shapes…impactful photographs…eye-catching titles…neat columns of text. Sound good? It should. These are most likely the reasons you picked up this book, and it's what you'll find within these pages.

But there's more—much more—to simply graphic scrapbook pages than paring down page embellishments and making everything neat and tidy. This refreshing new style is often inspired by print advertisements, billboards, CD jackets, magazine articles and other designs. And before those creations could grab a scrapbooker's attention long enough to inspire a layout, there were graphic designers hard at work on them, bringing all the elements together in pleasing arrangements.

Whatever the design, the primary goal of every graphic designer is to communicate a message, and to do so simply and clearly. Just like designers, scrapbookers want to create the perfect marriage of text and images. The only difference is the message—scrapbookers have the unique privilege of communicating their love for a new baby, the humor in a toddler's words, appreciation for a caring spouse or the excitement of travel. You know, the important stuff!

What's more, graphic designers are always honing their craft by attending seminars, seeking out critiques from other professionals in the field and reading inspiring publications. Sound familiar? We thought so. That's why this book includes information on tried-and-true design concepts that graphic designers have been using for years, in addition to a variety of clean and crisp layouts by many talented artists.

Lydia Rueger, Editor

why it works:
layout

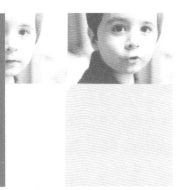

Further, in each chapter, you'll find a section called "Why It Works"—which dissects a page so one can see the thought process behind it. The breakdowns can serve as helpful checklists for your own page designs.

Simply Graphic is divided by concept, type, image and layout to help you focus on different aspects that are important in design. You'll be creating the graphic style you love with a designer's eye in no time. When others look at your pages and comment on the clean lines and impactful photographs, you'll smile, knowing it's really your knowledge of balance, rhythm, unity and other design principles that brings it all together.

To gain further insight on how to "keep it clean," we've enlisted the help of our own design department, who offer critiques titled "Designer's Eye" throughout the book.

Designer's
eye

I Love You

from the bottom of my

concept

Chances are you've seen certain scrapbook pages and commented to a friend, "Now that's a great idea!" The design is clean, the image is impactful, the message is clear, but there's something else that makes the page special. The great idea behind the page that made you stop and take notice means it has a strong concept. Great concept can be shown in a variety of ways, but one thing is consistent in all well-concepted pages: There's a preplanning stage in which the idea is developed long before the photos touch cardstock. And this stage is more than just deciding what page elements go where. It means brainstorming how you can turn that subject inside out to present it in a new and interesting way. For example, the photo sequence you took of your toddler and dog is cute, but wouldn't it be funny to invent a dialogue between the two of them? The scrapbook artists in this chapter illustrate strong concept through interesting photo perspectives, comparisons of personality traits, plays on words, humor, introspective moments, pages that depict the passage of time and more.

Document similar traits

1 Old and new photos were printed at the same size to emphasize physical similarities.

2 Ampersand placed to cover the edges of both photos creates a visual connection between the two.

3 Floral patterned paper lends an old-fashioned feel while stripes add a modern touch, much like the "vintage meets modern" page concept.

4 Circles with dates add clean dimension while highlighting the concept.

5 Curved angles surrounding the photos draw them together to form one central focal point.

my mother & my daughter

Fifty-five years separate these two photos. and these girls look like they could be twins. They have the same purity of face, the same mouth, the same hands, the same curly blonde hair.

One photo is a smiling girl with her whole life ahead of her, who later became my mother. I have seen what she's made of her life: she's a smart, educated woman who raised her family well and made her priorities clear through her quiet acts of love and service. The other photo is a smiling girl with her whole life ahead of her—and her story is still unwritten.

I am stunned by the thread of family symbolized by these two photos. Your grandma has given you a legacy—through me—of love and service, sacrifice and goodness, and the possibility and potential for you is endless. And I wonder, Rowen, who will you become?

1950

2005

WHO WILL YOU BECOME?

Using photos of her mother and daughter at the same age, Jessica created an introspective comparison of the two. Rather than creating a page that focused just on their physical traits, she went further to describe her mother's character in the journaling. For her daughter whose future is yet to be determined, Jessica mused about her potential.

My Mother & My Daughter
Jessica Sprague, Apple Valley, Minnesota

Supplies: *Patterned papers (Chatterbox); chipboard circles, textured cardstocks (Bazzill); dimensional glaze (Plaid)*

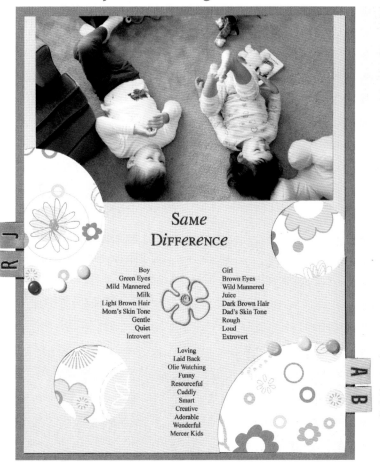

Becky chose a photo of her children lying side by side for a page that celebrates their differences and similarities. She listed differences below each child, then made a list of their shared characteristics in between. To further highlight their differences, she layered two patterns beneath her cardstock, then cut holes with a nested template so they would show through. Different colored initial tabs adorn each side.

Same Difference
Becky Mercer, Newark, Delaware

Supplies: *Patterned papers (Scrappy Cat); textured cardstocks (Bazzill); brads (Making Memories); fabric tabs (Scrapworks); wire flower (Maya Road)*

Same Difference

Boy	Girl
Green Eyes	Brown Eyes
Mild Mannered	Wild Mannered
Milk	Juice
Light Brown Hair	Dark Brown Hair
Mom's Skin Tone	Dad's Skin Tone
Gentle	Rough
Quiet	Loud
Introvert	Extrovert

Loving
Laid Back
Olie Watching
Funny
Resourceful
Cuddly
Smart
Creative
Adorable
Wonderful
Mercer Kids

Photograph a sequence

AUGUST 5, 2005

before............................during............................after

Isaac is just now old enough to start riding the big boy rides at the carnival.   He wanted me to ride this ride with him but I told him that I just couldn't force myself to get on that thing.....I would be too dizzy to walk after it was all over.   So, he braved it with another little boy. I was extremely worried when the thing was whipping around, but when I saw the big grin on Isaac's face during the whole ride, I knew he was okay and actually having fun. My baby is no longer a baby......he's a boy!

the **SCRAMBLER**

Ronnie photographed her son before, during and after his first ride on the "big boy" Scrambler to document the event. The repeated photos taken at different angles add the feeling of movement to the page. It also allowed Ronnie to capture her son's expression during all stages of the ride. For the background design, she altered a photo of a Ferris wheel with image-editing software.

The Scrambler
Ronnie McCray, St. James, Missouri

Supplies: *Image-editing software (Adobe Photoshop Elements 2.0)*

Danielle recorded her 6-month-old's schedule in a digitally rendered clocklike design. The layout allowed her to use many random snapshots she'd taken of her daughter, and the large, circular design element pulls them all together to give the page one central focus. Journaling describing each part of baby Zoë's day is printed underneath each photo. Photo anchors secure the photos' edges while allowing readers access to the journaling underneath.

Zoë
Danielle Catalano-Titus, Woburn, Massachusetts

Supplies: Image-editing software (Adobe Photoshop 7.0); photo anchors (source unknown); cardstock; pen

Depict a progression in nature

Margie showed a progression of sunrise and sunset by taking several photos at the same location at different times of day. The gradient effect applied to her title captures a similar feel. On the black background, the rising and setting sun stands out dramatically.

Sunrise to Sunset
Margie Lundy, Troy, Ohio

Supplies: Image-editing software (Adobe Photoshop)

Designer's eye

Kacie used a creative, interlocking grid to separate her birthday information. Setting the type on a vertical plane and enlarging key words also adds movement to static information.

Research birthday history

Kacie literally gave her concept a new angle when she used the same layout for either side of this spread. One side is simply the upside-down version of the other. The same-yet-different layout supports the concept of Kacie's and her husband's birthdays—in the same month and year, but on different days. Different colors of cardstock for bits of trivia help differentiate between topics. Rounded corners on the outer edges of two journaling blocks give the spread a polished look.

On the Day We Were Born
Kacie Liechty, Louisville, Kentucky

Supplies: *Patterned papers (EK Success); letter stickers (American Crafts); cardstocks; corner rounder; pen*

Michele's journaling puts an interesting spin on the idea that children grow up too quickly. Simply titled "When," her journaling is phrased in questions to document the growing independence of her son. For a creative title treatment, Michele cut letters from black cardstock, then placed the letter outline over patterned paper.

When
Michele Woods, Reynoldsburg, Ohio

Supplies: *Patterned paper (KI Memories); cardstocks*

When did you get freckles on your nose?

When did you start to say words like 'nocturnal' and 'fabulous'?

When did you become old enough to start preschool?

When did you start letting me take pictures of you?

When did you turn from a toddler into a little boy?

When did you stop wanting me to rock you to sleep?

When did that all happen? It happened in the blink of an eye. I have to remember to savor every moment, as they all pass much too quickly.

Build concept around a child's phrase

AUGUST 2, 2005

- one more Lego space ship to build

- one more time around the block on our bikes

- thirty extra minutes of tv

- one wonka chocolate bar each time you go to the grocery store with me

- a couple more pushes on the swing

- one more cup of chocolate milk (even though I said only 2)

- two bedtime stories instead of one

these are **just** little things that are big things to you!

Although sometimes frustrating to her, Kris realized that her son's frequent requests for "just one more" of certain things are a big part of his life at his age, and are important to him. She put a positive spin on his common requests by making "Just" the title of her layout, followed by a list of his favorites. Kris added interest to a clean and simple title by changing the color of the letter U and adding a shadow behind the letter.

Just
Kris Gillespie, Brandon, Florida

Supplies: *Patterned paper (KI Memories); acrylic flower (LazerLetterz); metal flower charms (Making Memories); ribbon (Fibers By The Yard); label maker (Dymo); corner rounder (EK Success); cardstocks*

FOUR WORDS THAT ARE USED

A **LOT** LATELY.

THE JOYS OF TODDLERHOOD.
GOTTA LOVE IT. MARCH 2005

Desiree drew attention to four words commonly heard from her son by adding them to a photo to create a partial frame. The very simple layout allows readers to focus on a single aspect of this boy's personality. A carefully chosen photo adds humor and playfulness, requiring little else to capture this precious moment in time.

No. Stop. Don't. Quit.
Desiree McClellan, Wichita, Kansas

Supplies: *Rub-on letters (Autumn Leaves); cardstocks*

Ann used a clever play on words for her title to represent photos of seafood taken while visiting Seattle. Far from the typical Space Needle and Starbucks shots, Ann's spread offers a different perspective of the city while focusing on her family's love and appreciation for good food.

See Food Seattle
Ann Hetzel Gunkel, Chicago, Illinois

Supplies: *Image-editing software (Adobe Photoshop); ribbon and tag embellishments (Gina Cabrera, www.ddecd.com)*

Her sons' mispronunciations of their Halloween costumes gave Cheryl material for a unique Halloween page concept. In addition, she recorded "facts" about the two characters as described by her sons. She brought closure to her journaling by ending it the same way she began, with the words, "just like Jake and Luke."

Draclia & Franklynstein
Cheryl Overton, Kelowna, British Columbia

Supplies: Patterned paper (KI Memories); textured cardstocks (Bazzill); photo corners (Canson)

some little known facts about
DRACLIA & FRANKLYNSTEIN
according to Jacob & Lucas

Coincidentally, they are brothers, just like Jake and Luke.
Franklynstein does NOT wear a shell like a turtle.
(and if mommy or daddy say that one more time he's going to get flusterated)
He does, however, wear fluffy boots.
Draclia is not just your everyday, average, run-of-the-mill, garden variety vampire.
He is DRACLIA, KING of the VAMPIRES. (said in a spooky voice, naturally)
They are both very fast runners - particularly when they have treat bags in their hands
and are going door to door on Hallween night.
They like to wrestle each other, again, just like Jake and Luke

Journal from a different perspective

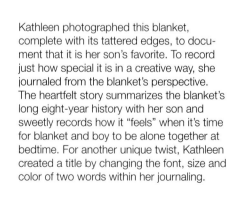

At first, you didn't really notice me, Drew. How could you? You were only a baby just starting to learn about the world around you. It was enough to be wrapped around you to keep you warm while you slept. Or to snuggle with you when you sucked your thumb.

Soon you began to recognize that I was always around. And if I wasn't, you noticed. There were some hard times when I had to take those detours to the washer and dryer.

When you started talking, you named me. No one is really sure how you came up with the moniker Owee (pronounced **OH**-wee). It's just what came out of your mouth. But it's the best name because there is no other blanket you call your Owee.

I've always looked forward to bedtime. Ok, maybe you complained sometimes that you didn't want to go to bed, but once the battle was lost for good and you had to concede defeat, it was time for you and me. Even better were the times you dragged me around with you while you were awake. And when the family took a trip, I came with you. I've traveled thousands of miles with you. And I'll travel thousands more with you if you wish. Now that we are

eight years

old. I'm a little tattered and worn. I wear those ragged edges with pride. Most of the time you still want me around. Like today. But there are times now when you forget about me. Surely there will come a time when there are more important things in your life and you won't think of me at all. That's ok. I'm just happy for the times we've shared and that no matter what, I will always be known as your favorite blanket.   Sept. 2005

Kathleen photographed this blanket, complete with its tattered edges, to document that it is her son's favorite. To record just how special it is in a creative way, she journaled from the blanket's perspective. The heartfelt story summarizes the blanket's long eight-year history with her son and sweetly records how it "feels" when it's time for blanket and boy to be alone together at bedtime. For another unique twist, Kathleen created a title by changing the font, size and color of two words within her journaling.

Eight Years
Kathleen Summers, Roseville, California

Supplies: Heart punch (EK Success); cardstocks

Designer's eye

Record a hobby with detail shots

There are thousands of scrapbooking supplies available in my local scrapbook store. But, each time I sit down to create a page, no matter what patterned paper or embellishments I intend to use, I always have the basics lined up on my desk. The necessary supplies I simply can't live without. The tools I need to complete a page. The "essentials" of my scrapbooking.

A favorite hobby was recorded in a bold, unique way when Becky photographed detail shots of the scrapbook tools she can't live without. She added variation to a repeated design pattern by placing the title vertically within the row of photographs. Journaling was tucked behind photos to keep the layout clean. Ribbons and tags add energy and playfulness.

Essentials
Becky Fleck, Columbus, Montana

Supplies: *Letter stickers (American Crafts); textured cardstocks (Bazzill); metal-rimmed tags, safety pins (Making Memories); jump rings (Junkitz); ribbons (Boxer Scrapbook Productions, Great Balls Of Fiber, Memory Creators); brass flower stencil (American Traditional Designs)*

Kristy demonstrated that her favorite color is lime by photographing all the different things in her home of that color. She grouped the photos close together to create an impactful splash of color for viewers. A clever title, playing off the popular phrase "living in the lime-light" adds pizazz to the page.

Living in the Lime Life
Kristy Nerness, Stanley, North Carolina

Supplies: *Image-editing software (Adobe Photoshop 7.0); brush tool (Rhonna Farrer)*

Allow a mishap to shape page concept

To document her son's marker mishap, Patricia designed a page made to look like someone had gone marker-crazy right on the layout. She changed the color of her background photos to give them the look of bright highlighter markers. She then added an "inked" digital overlay and used a digital brush to create scribble lines around her focal photo.

Marker Mayhem!
Patricia Richhart, New Haven, Indiana

Supplies: *Image-editing software (Adobe Photoshop CS); digital inked overlay (Tanya Todd-Krasen, www.scrapbookbytes.com)*

Highlight a hobby with examples

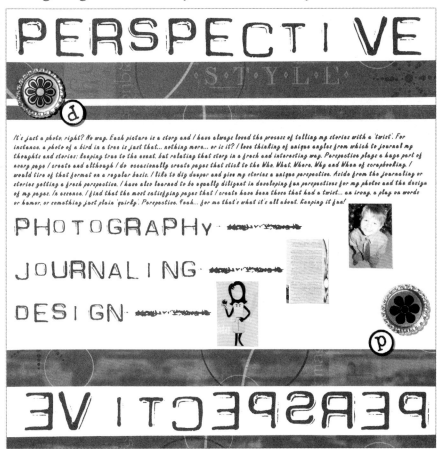

Ginger documents her love for scrapbooking in a nontraditional way. She journaled about how she loves to include fresh and interesting perspectives on her scrapbook pages rather than stick to the who, what, where, when and why of scrapbooking. Her bold and unusual layout and title printed backward illustrates her point exactly.

Perspective
Ginger McSwain, Cary, North Carolina

Supplies: *Patterned Paper (Autumn Leaves); bottle caps, bottle-cap stickers (Mustard Moon); round self-stick tags (EK Success); rub-on letters (Making Memories); cardstock*

Communicate mood with color

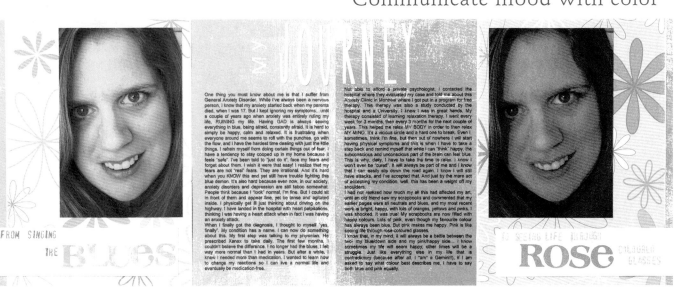

Caroline used color to further communicate a story of dealing with an anxiety disorder. The blue side of the spread, complete with a blue-tinted photograph, tells the story of Caroline's condition and how it started to control her life. The pink side of the spread talks about recovering from the condition and working to live a much happier life. Positioning the journaling through the center of the spread keeps the importance of the layout clear.

My Journey
Caroline Huot, Laval, Quebec, Canada

Supplies: *Patterned papers (Autumn Leaves, Basic Grey); letter stickers (Basic Grey, Chatterbox); rub-on letters (Making Memories); letter stamps (FontWerks); stamping ink*

Invent a conversation

Precious snapshots of her son and the dog were given a playful and funny twist when Linda wrote a "conversation" between the two. She went further with the concept by designing the page in a comic strip format, complete with a comiclike title. Simple, bold colors add to the playful feel while maintaining a clean appearance.

The Devious Duo
Linda Harrison, Sarasota, Florida

Supplies: *Letter stickers (Arctic Frog, Sticker Studio); textured cardstocks (Bazzill); rub-on stars (Basic Grey)*

The sad truth
It goes a lot like this:
what started out as just
a fun little place to go
has become one of my addictions
in recent years.
See I used to go to Target to
just window shop. I loved seeing
what was cool, what was in style
and what I just couldn't live
without. But in recent years,
It's like my inner shopping animal
has been unleashed. Every time I
step into Target, I become consumed
by the hunt for a deal. I scour the
clearance racks, look for stuff on
ad and load up my cart with everything
I want.

Mmm . . .

Target.

So I battle on
Trying to resist going to Target
for me is like keeping a kid
out of a candy store.
I just can't resist the deals
And the stuff.
I mean, really, where else
Can you get a cute little
Dog with a
Target-style eye?

addiction

A page about Teri's favorite store takes a fun twist when she documents it with an off-kilter picture of the Target dog. Simple cardstock blocks in Target's signature colors include humorous details about her love for the store. The title anchored by three guitar picks adds playfulness while keeping the focus on her journaling.

Addiction
Teri Anderson, Vancouver, Washington

Supplies: *Rub-on letters (Scrapworks); textured cardstocks (Bazzill); stamping ink; guitar picks; cardstock*

With the help of a drawing program, Joanna added words over her photograph to diagram the details of her son's changing table area. A nice photo of her husband and son is made more interesting and humorous as Joanna points out various details, including the fact that her son is still in his pajamas at 11:00 a.m. The haphazard style of the diagram is balanced with an ultra-clean title and journaling on solid tan cardstock.

Room With a View
Joanna Bolick, Fletcher, North Carolina

Supplies: *Image-editing program (Adobe Illustrator); rub-on letters (Making Memories); cardstocks*

Support concept with facial features

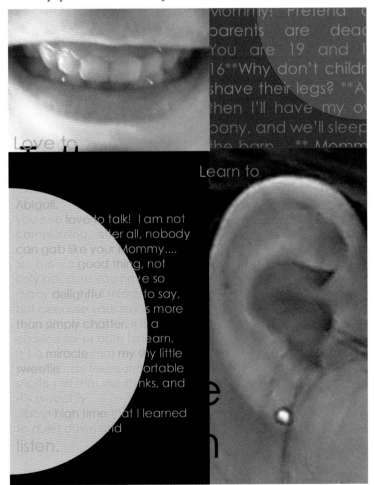

Elaine's layout documents her daughter's love of talking, but she also allowed the focus to shift to her herself and her desire to become a better listener. She wanted the journaling to be the focus of the page, so she included detail shots of an ear and a mouth to support the concept. Journaling in the upper right corner gives examples of her daughter's many questions and thoughts.

Love to Talk
Elaine Lang, Potomac Falls, Virginia

Supplies: *Image-editing software (Microsoft Digital Image Pro)*

One day while drawing with her son, Marla was inspired by an interesting diamond shape they created. She used a similar shape in her title, then played off the curves the diamond created to form the rest of the layout. The vertical curves help draw attention to a list of careers she'd like to try—the concept of her layout.

Top 20
Marla Kress, Cheswick, Pennsylvania

Supplies: Patterned paper (KI Memories); letter stickers (Mustard Moon); cardstock

Marla integrated a nice concept into the look of her layout by cropping the image on the "visual edge" of her top-20 list. By letting your eye make an imaginary line where a border should be, you can then design your page around those visual lines.

Mimi was sad when she got rid of two cars she'd had for a long time, so she said a final goodbye by creating a spread about them. She took pictures as each one was towed away, then accompanied those pictures with chronologies about both cars and all they'd been through. In negative space around each set of pictures, she added the name given to each car.

Sentimental Goodbyes
Mimi Schramm, Colton, California

Supplies: *Patterned paper (KI Memories); textured cardstocks (Bazzill); letter stickers (Sticker Studio, Wordsworth); bolt stickers (Sticker Studio); rub-on letters (Making Memories)*

Create a newspaper-style layout

Perhaps the granddaddy of graphic style, newspaper layouts, when backed by a strong, creative concept, are still a fun way to design a page. Susan created such a layout in the time leading up to her son's fourth birthday. While the birthday page itself will surely be chock-full of presents, guests and cake, Susan created this pre-party layout to focus on her son's current birthday "must-haves." She made a circle of red with image-editing software to mimic the look of a circled newspaper listing and to zero in on the focal point. All journaling was written in the style of classified ads to further support the newspaper concept.

Wanted: Birthday Party
Susan Cyrus, Broken Arrow, Oklahoma

Supplies: *Image-editing software (Adobe Photoshop); photo paper (Epson); cardstock*

To scrapbook about how often she seems to find herself on "red eye" overnight flights, Jennifer used a close-up picture of her eyes for a little play on words. The eye concept ties in to her journaling in yet another way in the last line: "And I remember why I travel. When that happens, it's not about red eyes at all. It's about a clear vision."

Red Eyes
Jennifer Lynn Moody, Lewisville, Texas

Supplies: *Patterned paper (Basic Grey); tags (Avery); distress ink (Ranger); fibers; transparency; pen; cardstock*

RED EYES

Friday, Feb 11 2005 5:47 am

Reno to DFW on American

on my way to CHA in Atlanta

I HATE THEM. ABSOLUTELY HATE THEM.

AND YET, I MANAGE TO FIND MYSELF ON AT LEAST A HALF—DOZEN A YEAR... AND THAT ISN'T COUNTING OVERNIGHT INTERNATIONAL TRIPS.

A TRUE RED—EYE LIVES UP TO THE NAME... A THREE TO FOUR HOUR FLIGHT THAT TAKES OFF AROUND MIDNIGHT PACIFIC TIME AND ARRIVES IN THE WEE BLEARY HOURS OF THE MORNING IN THE CENTRAL OR EASTERN TIME ZONE. YOU STAY UP LATE ENOUGH AND AWAKE EARLY ENOUGH (OR POSSIBLY DON'T SLEEP AT ALL) AND FIND YOURSELF MYSTERIOUSLY RUBBING YOUR EYES THE NEXT DAY.

USUALLY THERE IS A STORY BEHIND WHY I'M ON THE RED EYE. BECAUSE I WANTED TO HAVE A FEW EXTRA HOURS WITH FRIENDS ON A SUNDAY NIGHT AND STILL NEED TO BE AT WORK ON MONDAY. BECAUSE I HAD TO WORK ALL DAY FRIDAY AND DON'T WANT TO MISS A WEEKEND AT HOME. BECAUSE MY JOB REQUIRES ME TO BE IN TWO PLACES AT ONCE THAT HAPPEN TO BE 3000 MILES APART.

EVERY TIME I SWEAR I WILL NEVER DO IT AGAIN. AND YET SOMETHING AMAZING ALWAYS HAPPENS IN MY HEART WHEN I WALK OFF A PLANE AT DFW OR O'HARE OR DULLES OR JFK AT 5 AM. THE WORLD SLOWS TO A BLUR FOR A FEW MOMENTS. I CAN SEE AN ENTIRE INTERNATIONAL AIRPORT AWAKE. THE WORLD MOVES BY ME.

AND I REMEMBER WHY I TRAVEL. WHEN THAT HAPPENS, ITS NOT ABOUT RED EYES AT ALL • ITS ABOUT A CLEAR VISION.

Use multiple spellings for deeper meaning

from Haley's perspective.....

Sole Mates *soul mates*

...not the best photo, but it turned into great food for thought...

These soles tell a bigger picture - they are sturdy but well worn and broken in... a lot like our marriage - strong but comfortable, casual with no pretense. Reflections of who we are, why we work so well together, how we live. We live as soul mates, better together than apart - better entertwined and mingled than on our own. Like these soles, our souls are molded together, a great fit and impossible to replace.

A simple snapshot featuring Jodi's and her husband's shoes became the perfect visual to describe their relationship. She used the photo as an opportunity to include a play on words for the title. The spelling of "soul" was handcut from the same color cardstock as the background to hint at the true and deeper concept behind the layout. Jodi's journaling makes the connection between favorite shoes and a long relationship—broken in yet strong and comfortable.

Sole Mates
Jodi Amidei, Memory Makers Books

Supplies: *Patterned papers (Déjà Views); textured cardstock (Prism Papers); corner rounder (EK Success); pen*

A name became the concept of this page when Kim turned her son Quinn into a dictionary entry. She chose a photo that reveals his true spirit and personalized definitions of "Quinntessence" to pay tribute to her son.

Quinntessence
Kim Crothers, Ridgeland, Mississippi

Supplies: *Digital patterned papers (www.creativesnaps.com); image-editing software (Adobe Photoshop)*

QUINNtessence.

Q

quinn-tes-sence
Pronunciation: kwin-'te-s&n(t)s
Function: noun
1 : the essence of YOU in your purest and most lovable form
2 : the most typical example or representative
- quinn-tes-sen-tial
- quinn-tes-sen-tial ty

Create wishful layouts

Pontiac Solstice: A Pure Roadster | Curvaceous & Sleek | Designed for Action

July 2005

Pure Desire | The Thrill of the Open Road | Wind in My Hair | Music Blasting

Decisions | Decisions

They say timing is everything. Unfortunately, in this case it is. I need a new car ... this week. This one calls my name. Unfortunately, it's not due out ... until the Fall and there's a waiting list.

TIMING
is everything

Passion and exhilaration | Where there is a will, there is a way | I will find a way

Robin's layout centers around the concept of wishful thinking: This is the car she would like to have someday, even if the timing isn't right for now. She pulled photos of the car from the Internet and included shots from all angles, much like an advertisement. Her journaling style was inspired by write-ups she found while searching for the car. Her symmetrical design with all same-size photos works well to highlight various features of the car without letting one overshadow the others.

Timing Is Everything
Robin Cecil, Deltona, Florida

Supplies: *Image-editing software (Adobe Photoshop Elements 7.0); photographs (various Web sites)*

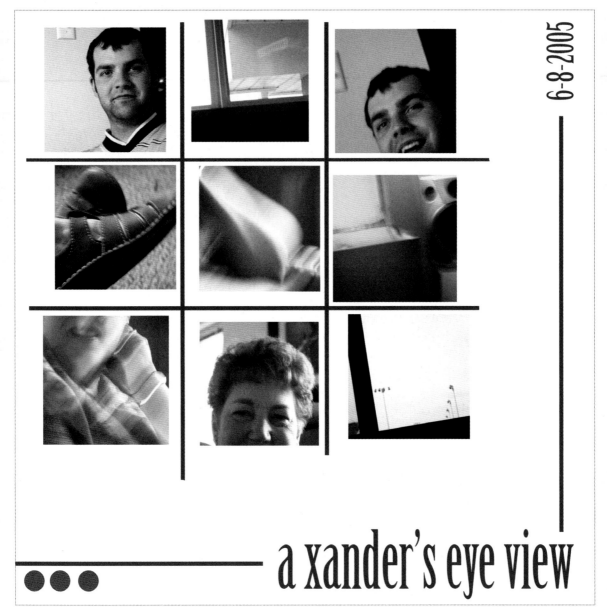

6-8-2005

a xander's eye view

Kara gives readers a glimpse into the world of her 2½-year-old son Xander by letting him get behind the camera instead of in front of it. She cropped the photos he took into equal-sized squares and added black lines between them to give a cohesive, linear feel—even if some are out of focus.

A Xander's Eye View
Kara Henry, Orem, Utah

Supplies: *Image-editing software (Adobe Photoshop CS)*

Linda reflected on her thoughts about public transportation on this neat and tidy page. She created lines on the computer and printed them on tan cardstock. She placed letters at the end of each line to simulate a subway map, which supported her page concept.

Public Transportation
Linda Harrison, Sarasota, Florida
Photo: Robert Harrison, Sarasota, Florida

Supplies: *Rub-on circles (Autumn Leaves); acrylic letters (source unknown); textured cardstock (Bazzill)*

Alter a movie poster idea

Patricia adapted a movie title and poster concept to document her son's potty training. In addition, she was inspired by an online scrapbook page titled "Mission Accomplished" for the completion of potty training. Since Patricia and her son had yet to overcome this hurdle, she changed up the angle to fit her situation. The graphic title coordinates with the boy's underwear in the photo, which she left in color while turning the rest of the photo black-and-white.

Mission: Impossible
Patricia Richhart, New Haven, Indiana

Supplies: *Image-editing software (Adobe Photoshop CS)*

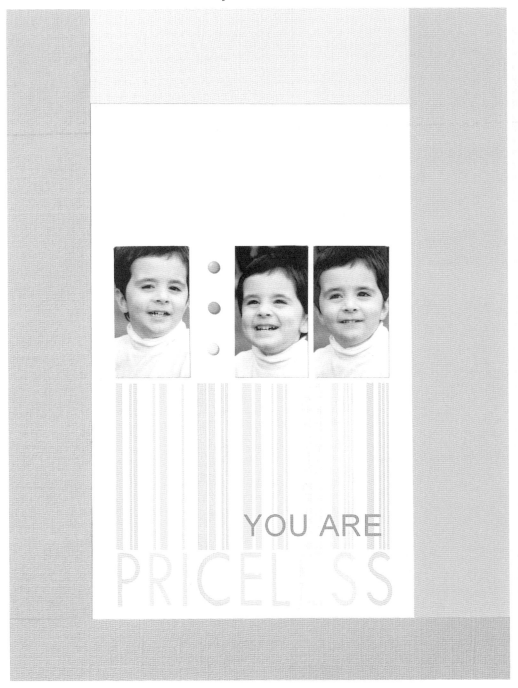

YOU ARE
PRICELESS

Desiree designed her page around the concept of combining a well-known credit card company's hallmark word "priceless" with a price-scan barcode for a page title. She printed her
barcode title directly onto cardstock, then framed the page in coordinating cardstock color
blocks for unity. To help her photos stand out on a white background, Desiree added coordinating brads in a vertical arrangement that mirrors the lines of the barcode.

You Are Priceless
Desiree McClellan, Wichita, Kansas

Supplies: *Textured cardstocks (Bazzill, National); fonts (Price Check, www.twopeasinabucket.com); mini brads (Lasting Impressions)*

Designer's eye

Ann has added a contemporary feel to the older subject matter of her layout. By placing a stylized, graphic list over an image, readability is lost—but the communication is not. This treatment is a new spin on the old "pointing arrow" technique.

Back up concept with retro style

Fonts and colors reminiscent of the 1920s were the perfect match for a layout featuring the craft room inside Ann's 1927 Arts and Crafts style home. A digital diagram placed over one of the photos offers details into how the craft room is organized. A list of the room's contents using the same number font as the diagram keeps the layout clean and easy to decipher.

Ann's Arts & Crafts Studio
Ann Hetzel Gunkel, Chicago, Illinois

Supplies: *Image-editing software (Adobe Photoshop 7.0); digital papers and accents (Design Butcher, www.scrapgirls.com)*

Represent a toddler's moods with objects

GOOD DAYS
BAD DAYS
IN-BETWEEN DAYS

SOME DAYS ARE GOOD. SOME DAYS ARE
JUST OK. SOME DAYS ARE BAD.
ALMOST 3 IS A STRANGE AGE. SOME DAYS
ARE FULL OF HUGS AND KISSES AND "YES
MUMMY." MOST ARE NOT. MOST DAYS ARE
SPENT NEGOTIATING TIME OUTS. AND THEN I
WALK OUT AND SEE YOU'VE LINED UP THE
FROSTED MINI WHEATS IN A NEAT ROW. AND
I JUST LAUGH. I SEE YOUR TRUCKS LINED UP
IN A NEAT ROW, I LAUGH. IT'S REALLY NOT
SUCH A BAD DAY AFTER ALL.

JULY 15, 2005

Treasure
the moment

To depict the challenge of parenting a 3-year-old, Linda photographed not the expressions of her son's face, but one of his quirks: lining things up in neat rows. She chose this perspective because once, after a particularly difficult day with him, it made her laugh when she saw he'd lined up his cereal in a row. These photographs remind her that he will only be little once, even if there are some bad days.

Good Days Bad Days...
Linda Buranasakorn, Irvine, California

Supplies: *Textured cardstocks (Bazzill, DieCuts with a View); phrase stamp (PSX Design); mini brads (Making Memories); label holder (Stampin' Up!); stamping ink; ribbon*

The title of Kim's page represents how much older she is than her husband, which provides a unique perspective for his 30th birthday layout. Circles behind her title and ages unify the page, while bright colors are appropriate for a festive birthday theme.

2 Years & 2 Days
Kim Mauch, Portland, Oregon

Supplies: *Digital papers and accents (www.theshabbyshoppe.com)*

Document a holiday differently

Linda poked fun at how easily eggs were hidden for her 2-year-old's Easter-egg hunt. No bunnies or baskets, just a simple purple arrow to highlight the "obvious" concept. To keep the background clean, she included her journaling on the arrows pointing to the egg.

The Obvious Egg
Linda Harrison, Sarasota, Florida

Supplies: *Patterned paper (Autumn Leaves); textured cardstocks (Bazzill); letter stickers (American Crafts, Doodlebug Design); hole punch (Fiskars)*

JULY 2005

STAŚ AT

To document her 4-year-old son's favorite things as well as some current facts-of-the-day, Ann divided this page into fourths. Each quarter consists of a photo of her son, digitally altered in different shades. The repeated element adds rhythm to the page while representing the boy's age through imagery.

Staś at 4
Ann Hetzel Gunkel, Chicago, Illinois

Supplies: *Image-editing software (Adobe Photoshop 7.0); digital papers and accents (www.scrapgirls.com)*

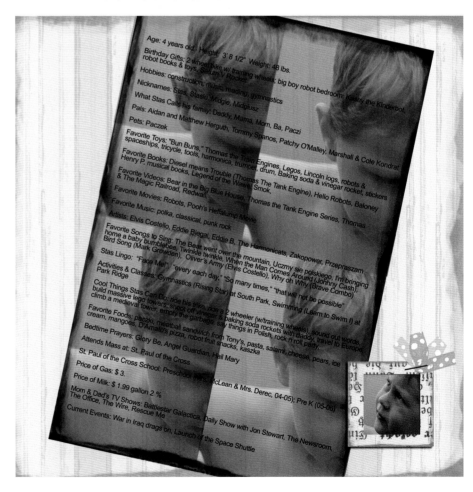

Age: 4 years old Height: 3' 8 1/2" Weight: 48 lbs.
Birthday Gifts: 2 wheel bike w/ training wheels, big boy robot bedroom, Kelsey the Kinderbot, robot books & toys, Saturn V Rocket
Hobbies: construction, music, reading, gymnastics
Nicknames: Staś, Stasio, Midgie, Midgiusz
What Stas Calls his family: Daddy, Mama, Mom, Ba, Paczi
Pals: Aidan and Matthew Herguth, Tommy Spanos, Patchy O'Malley, Marshall & Cole Kondrat
Pets: Paczek
Favorite Toys: "Bun Buns," Thomas the Train Engines, Legos, Lincoln logs, robots & spaceships, tricycle, tools, harmonica, trumpet, drum, Baking soda & vinegar rocket, stickers
Favorite Books: Diesel means Trouble (Thomas The Tank Engine), Hello Robots, Baloney Henry P, musical books, Legend of the Wawel Smok
Favorite Videos: Bear in the Big Blue House, Thomas the Tank Engine Series, Thomas & The Magic Railroad, Redwall
Favorite Movies: Robots, Pooh's Heffalump Movie
Favorite Music: polka, classical, punk rock
Artists: Elvis Costello, Eddie Biegaj, Eddie B, The Harmonicats, Zakopower, Przepraszam
Favorite Songs to Sing: The Bear went over the mountain, Uczmy sie polskiego, I'm bringing home a baby bumblebee, Twinkle twinkle, When the Man Comes Around (Johnny Cash), Bird Song (Mark Growden), Oliver's Army (Elvis Costello), Why oh Why (Brave Combo)
Stas Lingo: "Face Me!" "every each day," "So many times," "that will not be possible"
Activities & Classes: Gymnastics (Rising Star) at South Park, Swimming (Learn to Swim I) at Park Ridge
Cool Things Stas Can Do: ride his trike, ride a 2 wheeler (w/training wheels), sound out words, build massive lego towers, shoot off vinegar & baking soda rockets with daddy, travel to Europe, climb a medieval tower, empty the garbage, say things in Polish, rock n roll party
Favorite Foods: paczki, meatball sandwich from Tony's, pasta, salami, cheese, pears, ice cream, mangoes, D'Amato's pizza, robot fruit snacks, kaszka
Bedtime Prayers: Glory Be, Angel Guardian, Hail Mary
Attends Mass at: St. Paul of the Cross
St. Paul of the Cross School: Preschool with Mrs. McLean & Mrs. Derec, 04-05); Pre K (05-06)
Price of Gas: $ 3.
Price of Milk: $ 1.99 gallon 2 %
Mom & Dad's TV Shows: Battlestar Galactica, Daily Show with Jon Stewart, The Newsroom, The Office, The Wire, Rescue Me
Current Events: War in Iraq drags on, Launch of the Space Shuttle

Show action with a photo series

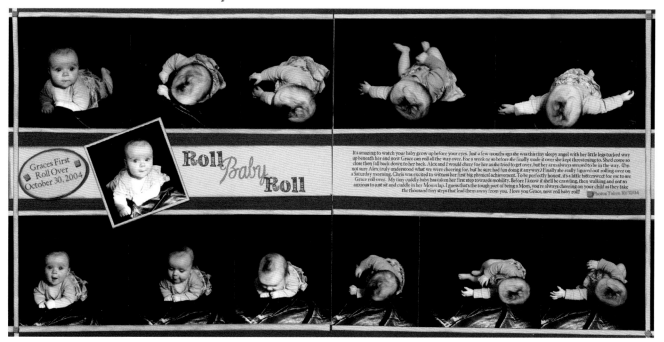

Lynn took shot after shot of her daughter to capture her first time rolling over. She placed the photos in sequential order to make it appear as if Grace is rolling right off the page. In an age where video cameras are standard, Lynn proves that you can capture action in your scrapbook as well with a little patience.

Roll Baby Roll
Lynn Brown, Boyds, Maryland

Supplies: *Square brads (Happy Hammer); textured cardstocks (Bazzill); chalk ink (Clearsnap); transparency*

Use multi-generational photos

For a page about a popular theme, Barb did more than show a photo of one loving couple. She showed what love looks like through three different couples, all at different stages of their lives: her sister-in-law, her husband's parents and a friend. No further journaling was needed to capture the idea of lasting love.

What Love Looks Like
Barb Hogan, Cincinnati, Ohio

Supplies: *Patterned paper, letter stickers, rub-on letters (Imagination Project); letter stamps (Hero Arts); embroidery floss (DMC); stamping ink; pens; cardstocks*

LiTTLE IliKebeinNgLITtlEiD
anTtogrOWUpi tOsTAy Tt
LiTTLeIli beinNgLItlEiDOn
wan togrOWUpiWAntOsTAyliT
LiTTLeIliKe beinNgLItlEiDOn
Ttog WUpiWAntt TAyliT
anT ogrO UpiWAntOs Ayli

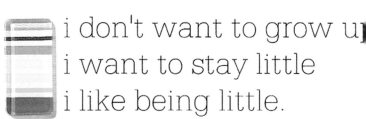

i don't want to grow u
i want to stay little
i like being little.

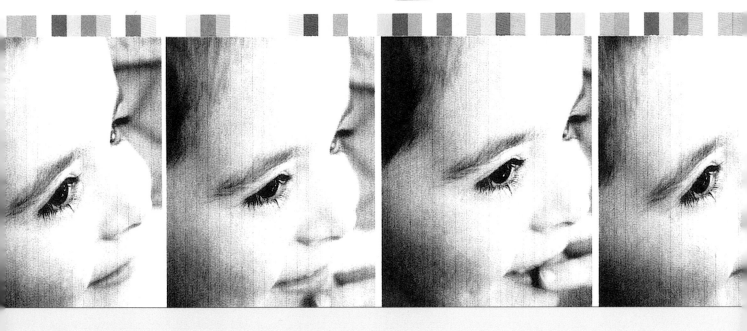

type

Using type effectively means more than remembering to journal or coming up with a catchy title. For graphic designers, the appearance of each letter is almost as important as what is being said. They select fonts that coordinate with the theme or mood they are trying to get across. Scrapbookers can do the same by taking cues from their photos. For example, a page featuring a vast, serene shoreline might coordinate with a light, airy script font. On the other hand, bold block letters could fit best with a photo of your husband. What's more, the way type is positioned on a page can easily contribute to a certain theme: A page titled "Close Ups" can feature letters that bump against one another. Whichever way you choose to present type, look at your photographs, think about the message you want to get across and display type to suit the individual needs of your content.

chapter two

why it works:
type

Give a title center stage ───────────────────────

1 A single colorful word amongst smaller, basic type creates a focal point.

2 White space draws attention to the type.

3 Short lines of text make for a quick and easy read.

4 Wide leading—the spaces between each line of text—gives journaling a clean, airy look and makes it easy to read.

5 The boy's face looking inward draws one's attention onto the page and toward the journaling.

6 Cardstock colors mimic letter colors, unifying the page.

spontaneous

③ Just recently you started giggling ...

④ Spontaneously that is. It's so weird. You'll be in bed and I'll hear you all of a sudden just start cracking up. I'm not sure what you're laughing at (or who) but it is humourous nonetheless. And it never fails to get me smiling too. From now on though we're going to have to call you "SG". Yea, I like the sound of that. What do you think?

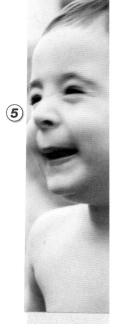

On a clean, white background, Desiree let the word "giggler" take center stage by using rub-on letters in different font styles and colors. The colors used in the word are picked up in cardstock colors around the edges to coordinate.

Spontaneous Giggler
Desiree McClellan, Wichita, Kansas

Supplies: *Rub-on letters (Making Memories); cardstocks*

Cheryl adjusted the kerning—which refers to the spacing between letters or characters in desktop publishing and typesetting—on the word "wide" so there is a significant amount of space between each letter. This keeps her type in line with her "wide open spaces" theme. She added lines to her text to convey a sense of motion along with the striped paper.

Wide Open Spaces
Cheryl Overton, Kelowna, British
Columbia, Canada

Supplies: *Patterned paper (Chatterbox); textured cardstocks (Bazzill)*

i've never met a kid who needs

w i d e

o p e n   s p a c e s

like this kid does.

Position type appropriately

I felt like such a nerd when I got my D70. I was wondering around my parent's house with manual and camera in hand. Whoever crossed my path was practically mauled and forced to pose. Sarah was quietly watching a movie in the kitchen until I sat down with my book. After about 50 photos, she started getting a little nuts. Perhaps she wouldn't have minded so much if it didn't take me forever to set up a shot.

A silly photo of a child is supported with the positioning of the title. Placed vertically and curved to fit with the circle-cropped focal photo, the title's placement conveys a fun-loving feel that is appropriate for Teresa's subject matter.

Silly
Teresa Olier, Colorado Springs, Colorado

Supplies: *Patterned paper (KI Memories); textured cardstock (Bazzill); flower brads (Making Memories); letter stickers (American Crafts)*

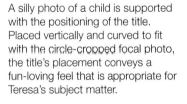

Designer's eye

By using a grid structure and leaving negative space around the images, Susan created that "clean and crisp" look. This is accentuated by her font choice— one that doesn't take away from the overall feeling of the layout. It is also important to keep text within the original grid structure for consistency.

Use one font in many sizes

fashionista
and she's not yet four

There are few things funnier than the differences between me and Bryn! Bryn, at three, has a better fashion sense than I have at 35. She loves glitter and pink and all things girly. I think it would be safe to say that I'm not that frilly. I know that we are going to learn a lot about negotiations and compromise together over the next 15 years. I know that I'll have to lighten up a bit and she'll need to learn to meet me part way. These pictures are a good example of one of our most recent negotiations. She wanted to wear her princess bathing suit to the hospital while I took newborn pics for a friend. It was too cold (and a bit much) so we came to an agreement - she would be allowed to wear the bathing suit over shirt and under jeans. Sure it looked a little weird to anyone without a 3 year old girl, but it worked! Now, let's see how we do in 12 years. I love you Brynne! 4-2-05

Using image-editing software, Susan added a number 4 for her daughter's age beneath her journaling. She adjusted the tint of the number so the journaling could be read easily. The ink colors were pulled from the photos for color harmony. A straightforward sans-serif font (a font with no tails on the ends of the letters) was used for legibility.

Fashionista
Susan Merrell,
Starkville, Mississippi

Supplies: *Image-editing software (Adobe Photoshop 7.0); textured cardstock (Bazzill)*

Change type styles for emphasis

Desiree balances her tightly cropped and rotated photos with simple color blocks with quotes upon quotes reflective of her page theme. The colors in the title and journaling are pulled from the paper blocks, creating a sense of harmony. Though the fonts vary in size, style and thickness, only sans-serif fonts were used, allowing them all to mesh together.

A Mind of One's Own
Desiree McClellan, Wichita, Kansas

Supplies: *Quote page (from Autumn Leaves book Quote, Unquote); cardstocks*

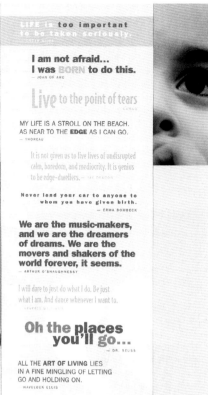

Design a dramatic starting letter

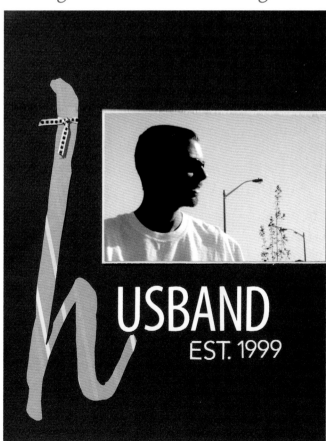

A strong initial lowercase letter adorned with a small ribbon adds color to Tracy's basic, bold husband page. The letter makes enough of a statement, along with the humorous "est. 1999" that little else is needed for impact.

Husband
Tracy Clements, Dunnville, Ontario, Canada

Supplies: *Patterned paper (Scenic Route Paper Co.); textured cardstock (Bazzill); letter stickers (Doodlebug Design); rub-on letters and numbers (Making Memories); ribbon*

Use bouncy type on a black background

Dimensional letters in lavender make a stand-out title over plain black cardstock. The focus stays on the precious photo of the little girl, while the color and random placement of the letters conveys a fun, youthful tone.

Fresh
Marie Cox, Springfield, Massachusetts

Supplies: *Patterned paper (Autumn Leaves); textured cardstocks (Bazzill); chipboard letters (Heidi Swapp); chipboard flowers, word tag (Making Memories); mini brad (Doodlebug Design)*

I look at you and am amazed that you are my child, my daughter. You are so perfect in every way and what is most surprising is that you are so unaware. Yes, you are a little diva, but you are not full of yourself and you are a very kind child. Your beauty is so fresh and I hope you always know that it matters most what's inside.

Position letters to fit concept

To illustrate the concept of standing strong, Jessica positioned the letters in the word as if they were standing. Although the font is basic, it is the placement of the word that makes the type enhance the design.

Stand Strong
Jessica Bellus, Tampa, Florida

Supplies: *Patterned paper (Autumn Leaves); textured cardstocks (Bazzill); letter stickers (American Crafts); rub-on letters (Scrapworks); preprinted transparency (Memories Complete); mini brads (Making Memories); ribbon (Offray); chalk ink (Tsukineko)*

Layer a "wet" title over a photo

A page of her son playing in the rain was given a true water-drenched effect with the title. With image-editing software, Ronnie used a layer style on her title font to give it a wet look. This also allowed her to include a horizontal photograph behind the title. Downloaded water droplets complement the title perfectly.

Wet James
Ronnie McCray, St. James, Missouri

Supplies: *Image-editing software (Adobe Photoshop Elements 2.0); water droplets (Denis Geromaine, www.e-scrappers.com); flower image (Computer Scrapping Elements 2 Yahoo Group)*

Bump title letters against each other

To get these shots of her dog, Cheryl had to get the camera up close to his face. Likewise, she placed her title letters for the word "close" up against one another to keep with the dog-in-your-face feel. Tiles with descriptions of the dog's face lend added detail.

Up Close
Cheryl Rohe, Baltimore, Maryland

Supplies: *Patterned paper (KI Memories); textured cardstock (Bazzill); mini brads (Jo-Ann Stores); ribbon (Offray); letter stickers (Imagination Project); rub-on letters (Doodle-bug Design); letter stamps (Hero Arts); tiles (Junkitz); stamping ink; pen*

Match title with main image

Chipboard title letters painted white contrast nicely with the background and enhance the close-up photograph of the lily. The thickness of the chipboard also adds a bit of dimension to the page. Melissa hand-stamped her journaling in black for a fun effect.

Lily
Melissa Godin, Lorne,
New Brunswick, Canada

Supplies: *Chipboard letters (Making Memories); textured cardstock (Bazzill); letter stamps (FontWerks); acrylic paint; stamping ink*

A magazine ad with a linear look and bold text inspired Brenda to create this page. She thought the color scheme would go nicely with photos from her motorcycle trip. A variety of bold, rugged fonts and a metal emblem on a black background were all the decoration her page needed.

The Open Road...
Brenda Becknell, Hamilton, Ohio

Supplies: *Foam alphabet stamps, rub-on letters (Making Memories); die-cut letters (Sizzix); Harley Davidson metal logo (EK Success); crackle stamp (JudiKins); distress ink (Ranger); cardstock; acrylic paint*

Use a fabric title label

Kelie's title serves double duty as an interesting design element. She chose a casual font for journaling that coordinates well with the premade fabric label title. The neutral background of the title serves as a nice contrast to the bright background.

Rest & Relax
Kelie Myers Brown,
Claremore, Oklahoma

Supplies: *Fabric label (source unknown); label maker (Dymo); brads; cardstocks*

Rustin is such a great uncle. I think he has more fun playing with the kids than the kids do playing with him! This one day, while up in Salmon, I caught him holding hand with Maddy and picking dandelions in the yard. They were so dang cute, so I grabbed my camera and got in on the action. When Rus showed Maddy how to blow the seeds into the air she was thrilled. She would blow as hard as she could (not really having much luck) then let Uncle Rus have a turn. It is so cute to hear her say, "Here Wustin!" 7.4.05

Lisa turned her title into a fun graphic element with a little help from a word-processing program. First, she created a ring of text on the computer and printed it on green cardstock. Then, she traced a premade chipboard letter "d" onto patterned paper, trimmed it and placed it inside the circle. A strip of the same striped paper running down the left side balances the weight of the graphic element.

Dandelions
Lisa Stephenson, Manteca, California

Supplies: *Patterned paper, die-cut square embellishments (KI Memories); textured cardstock (Bazzill); snaps, chipboard letter (Making Memories); text-editing program (Microsoft Word Art)*

Designer's eye

Lisa created correspondence by repeating the patterned paper in the border and for the letter "d." Using design elements like this sparingly give the layout that "less is more" look. Add in a bold background color with a few choice photos and the end result is a nicely balanced page.

Frame a photo with words

Casey & Ashley
Prom 2005

Type can serve as a photo frame while still maintaining a clean, graphic feel. Colleen's title does just that. The "And B" enclosed in a circle successfully balances the layout against the patterned paper circle in the lower left-hand corner. And when using a photo that isn't enlarged, surrounding it with type can make it appear larger and draw more attention to the focal point. Colleen created the title in Microsoft Word and printed it directly on gray cardstock.

See and B Seen
Colleen Adams, Huntington Beach, California

Supplies: *Patterned paper (Basic Grey); textured cardstock (Club Scrap); ribbon, ribbon slide (Making Memories)*

Add dimension to an initial

When Jennifer saw this photo of her children with their great-grandfather, she noticed the "W" shape that formed between their clasped hands—the same letter that begins their last name. She carried out the "W" theme with type by stamping and cutting the letter from foam. Her journaling talks about honoring the name of Wilmarth, which is supported by the strong initial.

Wilmarth
Jennifer Wilmarth, Ypsilanti, Michigan

Supplies: *Patterned paper (My Mind's Eye); textured cardstock (Bazzill); ribbon (Offray); Styrofoam paper (Dow Chemical Co.); letter stamps (Heidi Swapp); distress ink (Ranger); stamping ink*

WILMARTH

Sam and Katy-

I love this picture of you and Grandpa Wilmarth, even though the circumstances surrounding it were sad. We had just held Grandma Wilmarth's Memorial service. Grandpa kept repeating what a comfort it was to him to have you there. As I look at this picture the symbolism of his holding the hands of the future of the Wilmarth family was not lost on me. I am struck by how lucky you are to know such a great man and to carry his name. I hope that you are always able to honor that name which he has passed on to you.

Love, Mom

April 6, 2005

Place type to create a border

These **boots** are made for walkin'

This week, you and I went school shopping for the very first time. We went without your sister because I wanted this to be very special for you, just as it was for her. On the way there, you kept chanting, "Go... go, mommy... Go!" Then you asked, "How do you spell "Go"? I said, "G – O." You repeated, "G – O"... and then what? I said, "That's it. Just G – O." You thought about that and then said, "Well... that's not impressive!"

Well, darling, "G – O" might not be impressive, but this outfit you picked out for school sure is! All the way home we sang the song, "These boots are made for walkin' " over and over.

and that's just what they'll do. One of these days

these **boots** are gonna walk all over YOU!

Because the enlarged photo of her daughter in her new school outfit was so bright, Karen chose a clean, white background. This allowed her to make a page border out of type. By using two different, playful fonts and arrows, she proves that a border of type can be just as energetic and eye-catching as one made of shapes, lines or other accents.

These Boots Are Made for Walkin'...
Karen Buck, West Chester, Ohio

Supplies: *3-D stickers (American Traditional Designs); ribbon (Offray); metal tag (American Crafts); rub-on letters (KI Memories, Making Memories); cardstock*

Kathy made her title into a design element by positioning single words inside colorful circles. She designed the words on the computer and printed them directly onto white cardstock. The repetition of circles in the same colors as her patterned paper unifies the page.

Dog Days of Summer
Kathy Thompson Laffoley, Riverview,
New Brunswick, Canada

Supplies: *Patterned paper (Scrapworks); cardstock*

Stack text in a house shape

Type stacked and arranged in the shape of a house is a fitting design choice for a page about a home. Type is further used to enhance this layout through the letter G placed above the chimney, to represent both smoke and the artist's last name. Translucent letters allow the house to show through the type.

Home Is Where the Heart Is
Ann Hetzel Gunkel, Chicago, Illinois

Supplies: *Image-editing software (Adobe Photoshop 7.0); digital tab (Design Butcher, Coffee Talk Collection, www.scrapgirls.com); papers (Design Butcher, Cafe Sorbet Collection, www.scrapgirls.com)*

White script lettering over a multi-colored patterned background adds an additional decorative touch to Katie's Italian travel spread. She created the background by first scanning in vintage pinup images as well as some she sketched herself. She then assembled the images and chose colors using image-editing software, typed words over the design and printed it on cardstock so the words were "built in" to the background design.

Cinque Terre Italia
Katie Kaapcke, San Diego, California

Supplies: *Metal border strip and corners, metal-rimmed frame (Making Memories); textured cardstock (Bazzill); rhinestones (Magic Scraps); glass jewels (Mrs. Grossman's); stickers (Paper Adventures); image-editing software (Adobe Photoshop); dimensional adhesive (Duncan); metal charm (source unknown)*

The five towns on the Italian Riviera, Riomaggiore, Manarola, Corniglia, Vernazza & Monterosso al Mare. Dennise & I stayed in Vernazza, which after hiking the cliffs through the five towns was our favorite. Climbing the seemingly endless stairs to Corniglia was definitely an experience! I wasn't sure we were going to make it but, I have to say, it was worth it! Dennise introduced me to the most amazing invention of all time here, PESTO! Pesto I discovered comes from the Genova region, which is very near to the Cinque Terra. We had pesto soup, pesto pasta & the ultimate, pesto, tomato & fresh mozzarella sandwiches! The local people of these towns were so kind & friendly. Dennise & I met a lovely older Italian couple who ran a store in Moterosso & they told us all about the wines of the region. they gave us a great deal on the wine we purchased. Each town makes a label white wine and there is a Cinque Terre wine as well. They are also famous for their sweet dessert wine, "Sciacchetra". We of course felt it our duty to sample them all! Dennise & I rented this gorgeous "room", it was HUGE, with shuttered windows that opened out to the one main street through town. It was a paradise, one of my absolute favorite places in Italy and we didn't want to leave.

Pair script and large serif fonts

A large bold serif font in gray overlaid with a small script style in black allows each set of words to stand out equally, but differently. Together, the two form a design element while keeping the focus on the action-packed photo.

Carpe Diem
Margie Lundy, Troy, Ohio
Photo: ACE Adventure Center/Whitewater
Photography, Oak Hill, West Virginia

Supplies: *Image-editing software (Adobe Photoshop)*

Enhance a column of text with two fonts

Jaana breaks up text in a long column by using two distinctly different font styles. She alternated the two, choosing the script style for key descriptions she wanted to highlight.

Free
Jaana Olsen, Raymond, Alberta, Canada

Supplies: *Image-editing software (Adobe Photoshop Elements 3.0)*

Add letters over photos

Heather's photos, cropped into four narrow, vertical strips, create backdrops for her title letters. Positioned near the bottom of each photo, the bright orange letters create impact while not overshadowing her precious black-and-white shots. The page was inspired by a billboard she saw when driving home one night.

Mommy's Boys
Heather L. Graham, Chandler, Arizona

Supplies: *Patterned paper (Karen Foster Design); rub-on letters (Making Memories); ribbon (May Arts); cardstock; acrylic paint; pen*

Decorate a background with words

Various sports-related words arranged between photos form a background design for Dana's T-ball page. Acrylic letters, clear-backed stickers, letter stamps and pieces cut from patterned paper all come together to create a rugged, boyish feel.

T-Ball
Dana Swords, Doswell, Virginia

Supplies: *Patterned paper (Frances Meyer, Rusty Pickle); template (Deluxe Designs); word stickers (Creative Imaginations, Deluxe Designs); letter stamps (All Might Media, EK Success, Making Memories); acrylic paint; stamping ink; cardstock*

BA
SE
BA
LL

It's so great

you found a sport

you love to play.

Cooperstown 2004

Betsy got the idea for her title and journaling arrangement from a magazine article. The large black letters form her title, "Baseball," while the journaling is sandwiched in between. Together, the journaling and title create a design element that balances Betsy's photo montage.

Baseball
Betsy Sammarco, New Canaan, Connecticut

Supplies: *Patterned paper, conchos, preprinted words (Scrapworks); textured cardstock (Bazzill)*

Designer's eye

Betsy used a grid structure to showcase many different angles and sizes of photos in this layout. In doing so, she adds variety in an organized fashion. Working the title into the grid is the final touch, giving the layout a tight yet balanced feel.

a first love

rekindled

Josh has always loved Parker Smith. They were in the same class at Northbrook Church and played together at her house during our Bible study every Sunday night. I'm not sure if he liked her so much because she was so cute, or fun, or had great toys to play with. But he's always called her his girlfriend. She already had a little boy playmate in Riley Hooper, but Josh didn't care. Parker was his girlfriend and he would marry her one day. When we moved he was so sad to leave her. He finally got to see her after over a year and didn't recognize her at first. It didn't take long though. He and Riley fought over who would sit by her. Josh said well she's my girl-friend so I should. They were so cute together. Love, it's a beautiful thing.   Jan '04

A wash of translucent color cascading down from the word "rekindled" creates a clean canvas for Margie's journaling. The title word, in a romantic, flowing script, suits the page theme and draws attention to the story below. Faded text behind the silhouetted subjects enhances the background.

A First Love Rekindled
Margie Lundy, Troy, Ohio

Supplies: *Image-editing software (Adobe Photoshop)*

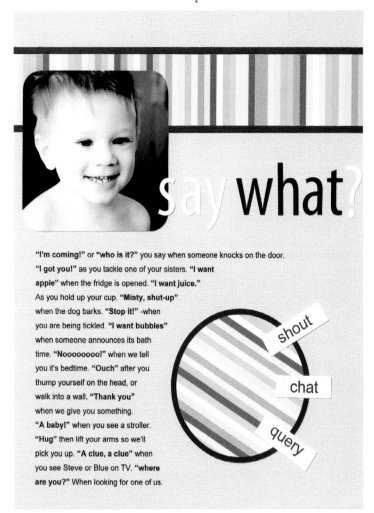

Teresa recorded her son's common sayings on a clean, graphic layout. She made her son's words bold to make them stand out from the rest. A circular design element including more words accents the chatty theme.

Say What?
Teresa Olier, Colorado Springs, Colorado

Supplies: *Patterned paper (KI Memories); textured cardstocks (Bazzill); letter stickers (Doodlebug Designs); corner rounder (EK Success)*

say what?

"**I'm coming!**" or "**who is it?**" you say when someone knocks on the door. "**I got you!**" as you tackle one of your sisters. "**I want apple**" when the fridge is opened. "**I want juice.**" As you hold up your cup. "**Misty, shut-up**" when the dog barks. "**Stop it!**" -when you are being tickled. "**I want bubbles**" when someone announces its bath time. "**Noooooooo!**" when we tell you it's bedtime. "**Ouch**" after you thump yourself on the head, or walk into a wall. "**Thank you**" when we give you something. "**A baby!**" when you see a stroller. "**Hug**" then lift your arms so we'll pick you up. "**A clue, a clue**" when you see Steve or Blue on TV. "**where are you?**" When looking for one of us.

shout

chat

query

Tear the center of a title

Smile

If you can't lift the corners, let the middle sag.

Photo taken by Ricky ~ June 2005

By tearing the center from her title and adhering a strip of journaling behind it, Yolanda accomplished several things: She made her title into an interesting design element, made room for journaling in a compact space and mimicked the idea of a open-mouthed smile. To create the word "Smile," Yolanda printed out the word in an outlined font and painted inside the lines with purple.

Smile
Yolanda Williams,
Charlotte, North Carolina

Supplies: *Patterned papers (American Crafts); textured cardstocks (Bazzill); acrylic paint; pen*

Highlight a word with an embellishment

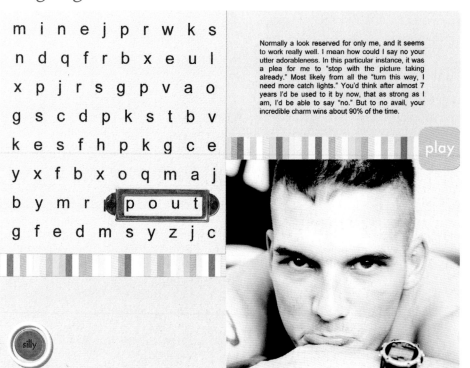

m i n e j p r w k s
n d q f r b x e u l
x p j r s g p v a o
g s c d p k s t b v
k e s f h p k g c e
y x f b x o q m a j
b y m r [p o u t]
g f e d m s y z j c

Normally a look reserved for only me, and it seems to work really well. I mean how could I say no your utter adorableness. In this particular instance, it was a plea for me to "stop with the picture taking already." Most likely from all the "turn this way, I need more catch lights." You'd think after almost 7 years I'd be used to it by now, that as strong as I am, I'd be able to say "no." But to no avail, your incredible charm wins about 90% of the time.

play

silly

A metal label holder and brads were used to zero in on the theme of the page in a sea of random letters. Teresa got the idea from a sheet of word search-style patterned paper that she saw. But when the paper didn't include the word she was looking for, she made her own on the computer, allowing wide spaces between letters and words to make room for the embellishment.

Pout
Teresa Olier, Colorado Springs, Colorado

Supplies: *Patterned paper, metal word, preprinted word square (KI Memories); textured cardstock (Bazzill); mini brads (Doodlebug Design); concho (Scrapworks); label holder (source unknown)*

Create an acronym

Mikki's creative title also serves as an acronym for words describing her son's personality. The letter "E" lifts to reveal journaling beneath, keeping the design clean and linear while still including the details behind her son's unhappy face. Photos of her son arranged in an uneven, overlapping pattern create balance with the similarly arranged title letters.

Oh...Dear
Mikki Livanos,
Jacksonville, Florida

Supplies: *Patterned paper (Imagination Project); textured cardstocks (Bazzill); rub-on letters (Making Memories); distress ink (Ranger); pen*

Oh...
D E A R
is for Dirty
is for Energetic
{LIFT}
is for Athletic
is for Rowdy

Add a glowing title

Luminarium

I had gone to the Luminarium in Merrion Square with people from the lab last year so when I saw a different one had come back as part of St Patrick's festival I knew I wanted to go. It's the most amazing thing, a giant inflatable structure of interconnecting tunnels and chambers all made of plastic and zipped together. All the colours are due to the sun shining through the plastic from the outside so they change as the weather does. Everything is rounded and there are funny little projections from the chambers where you can just sit and look around. The central chamber is full of pillars and the roof looks as if it has stars, small recesses glow with incredible brilliance. It had been down on a platform near the IFSC all week and Sunday was my last chance to go and see it. I went to Geoff's first for tea and crumpets with some friends of his and then Geoff, Dave Kate and I walked across. Unfortunately we hadn't booked so we had to queue and queue but we agreed we didn't have anything to do that afternoon and we finally got into the very last session of the day. People automatically speak in quiet voices in there and we wandered from room to room or sat peacefully in the recesses. Because we were the last out we watched them deflate it after us, it all shrank down to nothing very quickly. I hope it becomes as much a part of the festival as the Skyfest fireworks, this year's were as good as always, Laura, Elaine, Kevin, Cormac and I watched from in front of the Custom House and agreed that the timing to music was better than ever.

To accompany photos taken inside the Luminarium, an inflatable structure of tunnels that results in interesting lighting effects, Emma designed a glowing title. She used a gradient rainbow effect from Microsoft Word Art, then filled the background of her text box with black and printed on glossy paper. Her journaling in white also supports the illuminated theme of the experience.

Luminarium
Emma Finlay, Sutton, Dublin, Ireland

Supplies: *Word-processing program (Microsoft Word); cardstock*

Designer's eye

When layering two boxes of text, the designer must choose fonts carefully so that both lines of type can be read easily. By applying a color gradient to a large serif font and layering it with a fine-lined script in black, Nikki's title is easy to read and creates a successful focal point.

Weave a quote through a title

imagine

Everything you can imagine is real.

Pablo Picasso

dream...look closer...find the artist inside you...ask questions
listen...think deeper...search for beauty
create...be inspired, for you are an exquisite work of art.

Nikki got the idea for this layout from an advertisement in a home decorating magazine. She then gave it her own spin by weaving a quote through her title. The title is proof that type can be a successful focal point while still having room for a variety of photos, journaling details and open space.

Imagine
Nikki Merson, Troy, Missouri

Supplies: *Patterned paper, letter stickers (Creative Imaginations); textured cardstock (Bazzill)*

riley

It is miraculous — to see what you create... it is a gift to be part of your world.
xoxo Mommy

miss you

I am no superman.
I have no reasons for you.
And I am no hero,
oh that's for sure.
But I do know one thing:
Where you are is where
I belong.

"My hands were made for holding you
and the girls, not a gun."
--Brad 2004

november 2003

Type was kept simple to keep the focus on a photo of an emotional time—the day before Dorothy's husband left for Iraq. So the title could extend over the photo, Dorothy turned the second word white so it could be clearly seen on the dark background. Song lyrics and a sentence her husband wrote in a letter make up the journaling.

Miss You
Dorothy Huffmanparent,
Moore, Oklahoma

Supplies: *Image-editing software (Microsoft Digital Image Suite); lyrics (Dave Matthews, Where Are You Going?)*

Arrows interspersed with Sue's title along with the gentle curve of the words contribute to the idea of giving back to others. Worn and rustic-looking letter stickers work well with the content of Sue's photos—her son helping with and showing hogs at the 4-H fairgrounds. Journaling about her son's involvement with 4-H is hidden behind the top photo to keep the design clean.

Giving Back
Sue Fields, South Whitley, Indiana

Supplies: *Patterned papers (Junkitz); chipboard numbers (Li'l Davis Designs); letter stickers (Bo-Bunny Press); die-cut arrows (QuickKutz); fasteners (Destination Scrapbook Designs); cardstock*

Turn a letter into a photo montage

To create a page about her unusual last name, Tracey turned the first letter of the name into a large design element. She cut an "O" from patterned paper, then using her publishing software, created and printed a photo montage in the same shape. Other letters in her last name were added inside the large "O." Above and below the design in opposite corners, Tracey typed two common questions people ask about her name.

Odachowski
Tracey Odachowski, Newport News, Virginia

Supplies: *Patterned paper (SEI); textured cardstocks (Bazzill); letter stickers (KI Memories); image-editing software (Microsoft Picture It!); pen*

Select fitting fonts

Ronnie wanted to give a photo of her son playing with sparklers the look of an old-fashioned poster advertising magicians. She achieved this through the selection of specific fonts. The date, placed with wide kerning along the bottom, also adds to this theme.

Matthew the Amazing
Ronnie McCray, St. James, Missouri

Supplies: *Image-editing software (Adobe Photoshop Elements 2.0)*

...acey documented the first time she heard that common question uttered by children on road
...e by making it the title of her page. Handcut paper letters in different styles and a large "@"
...gn to start the question makes the title a fun and interesting design element all its own.

...e We There Yet?
...acey Odachowski, Newport News, Virginia

...plies: Patterned paper, stickers, premade shapes (KI Memories); textured cardstocks (Bazzill); letter stickers (Chatterbox); word tiles
...Davis Designs); pens

Tia repeatedly stamped the word "cry" to emphasize the many times a day that a young child cries to get attention. She overlaid her page with a paper cut-out, stamped, then re-moved the cut-out so the word would not overlap the space she'd allowed. For variation within the repeated element, Tia outlined one of the words with a black pen.

Cry
Tia Bennett, Puyallup, Washington

Supplies: *Textured cardstock (DieCuts with a View); letter stamps (FontWerks); number stamps (Making Memories); ribbon (May Arts); stamping ink; pen; staples*

Angle type to draw the eye

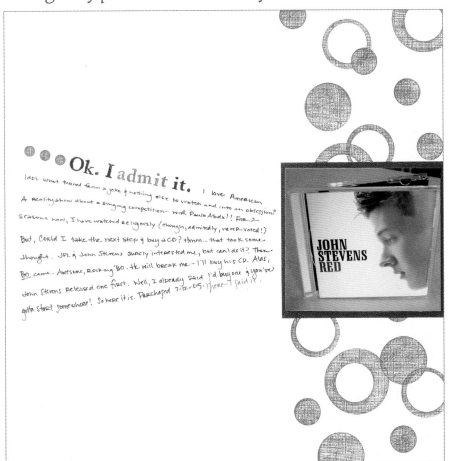

The angle of Tracey's journaling provides a unique look while allowing the viewer's eye to be drawn into the focal point. While the angle of the words draws you to the photo, it also gives the appearance of "music" radi-ating from the photo of the CD. She repeated the use of the color red to coordinate with the CD cover.

OK. I Admit It.
Tracey Odachowski,
Newport News, Virginia

Supplies: *Textured cardstock (Bazzill); circle and letter stamps (Stampin' Up!); stamping ink; pen*

Make a bold statement with simple type

The contrast of bold, black letters on a white background is always a simple yet effective way to add impact through type, as Celeste's page demonstrates. She chose shiny, black metallic premade letters to echo what her son was saying in the photo. A line of small rub-on dots running from the photo to the title tie the two together.

ooh! that's exactly what you are saying here. now you are probably wondering what the ooooh-ing is all about. it's nothing exciting really...to get you to look at the camera [a nearly impossible task,] daddy is holding a big chocolate chip cookie over mommy's head. guess that is one of the things that make you go ooh!

OOH

OOH
Celeste Smith, West Hartford, Connecticut

Supplies: *Metal letters (American Crafts); rub-on dots (KI Memories); ribbons (KI Memories, May Arts); cardstocks*

Balance title against the focal point

One's eye goes to the black title almost as quickly as it goes to the photo of the boys on a sled. By placing the title in the lower right corner, Cheryl successfully balanced her focal photo. She positioned the title so that it serves as the last word of a quote as well. Adding all type to the lighter shade of gray cardstock allows it to stand out.

Fly
Cheryl Overton, Kelowna, British Columbia, Canada

Supplies: *Textured cardstocks (Bazzill); letter stickers (American Crafts); ribbon (Offray); mini brads (Making Memories)*

Jake & Big Luke
December 2004

If I could pick a **superpower,** I would choose to... fly

Together, a simple serif font and a script font in a larger point size make up this quote to complement Lisa's photograph. By limiting her font styles to just two, Lisa was able to make a stronger statement with type and enhance the serene quality of her photo. The large field of open space surrounding the quote makes it stand out even more.

Torrey Pines 2002
Lisa Howell, Tucson, Arizona

Supplies: *Digital papers (Sand & Surf kit by Holly McCaig, www.thedigichick.com)*

Contrast black letters with a white background

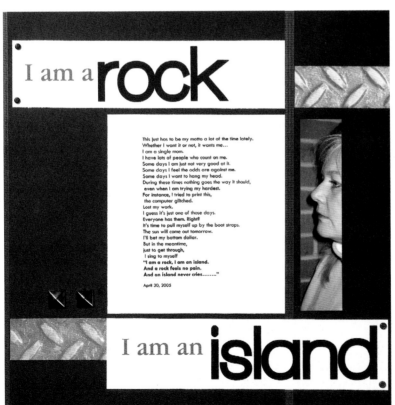

With just a sliver of a photo peeking from the right side of this page, it needed a rock-solid title to anchor it. To balance the page, Heide included song lyrics along the top and bottom in identical, bold fonts. In addition to balancing the page, the steady, strong fonts are indicative of the kind of person she feels she must be, as described in her journaling.

I Am a Rock...
Heide Lasher, Englewood, Colorado

Supplies: *Patterned paper (Provo Craft); mini brads (Jo-Ann Stores); cardstocks; lyrics (Paul Simon, I Am a Rock)*

Designer's eye

Text formatted on a curve supports the images chosen for this layout. Short columns successfully break up the large amount of text, making it easier to read. That shape connects the reader's eye to the next set of text—a unique visual bridge that gives this layout an extra spark.

Format journaling in curved shape

In 1958 when Daddy was in the Navy stationed in Iwakuni Japan, he had the opportunity to shop at the Army Post Exchange in Yokosuka. His brother-in-law Bob, who was in the Air Force, had gone there a couple years earlier and had bought his wife (Dad's sister Angela aka "Babe") a set of Noritake china in the Silvine pattern. One of Dad's other sisters, Moira, wanted the same dishes since they were so beautiful and also so that if she and Babe ever threw a party together they'd have enough of the same dishes for everyone. So Dad bought a set for Moira. The dishes had to go from the Exchange to Iwakuni and then to Alameda, California, the location of Dad's squadron. When Dad went on leave, he drove the china across the country to Montclair, New Jersey where Moira lived. For many years, Moira and her family enjoyed the china on special occasions and lovingly washed each piece after each use, carefully placing them back in their original packaging.

Sometime around 1995, Moira moved to a farm in Broadbacks, Pennsylvania and since there was no need for china on the farm, Rennie, one of Moira's daughters, took the china with her to her hometown in Long Island, New York and put them in storage.

In 2002 Moira passed away and Dad went back east for the funeral. Moira's daughters (my cousins) Rennie and Suzy decided that Dad should have the china back to "give to one of his daughters". At the time, my two sisters were doing quite well for themselves and had many nice things and Dad decided that my family would be the most blessed by having the china. A few months later when Dad was back in the area for a reunion with some old high school buddies and he could manage the logistics, he picked up the china from Rennie in New York and drove it back with him to Blairstown, New Jersey where he was staying with his buddy Jonesy. From there he had each piece wrapped carefully (with $94 worth of packaging materials!) and Fed Ex'd the dishes to me in Rocklin, California. In 2005 Suzy discovered a few more pieces and sent them to me in June to our new home in Roseville, California.

Whew! What a travel over time and distance to get to us! It makes this china even more special to us... it's now officially a family heirloom!

47 years, 11,056 miles, and the birth of a family heirloom

1958 Dad purchases china in Yokosuka, Japan

561 miles from the Exchange to Iwakuni, Japan

5,437 miles from Iwakuni, Japan to Alameda, CA

2,553 miles from Alameda, CA to Montclair, NJ

15 miles from Montclair, NJ to Long Island, NY

55 miles from Long Island, NY to Blairstown, NJ

2,435 miles from Blairstown, NJ to Rocklin, CA

2005 Cousin Suzy sends the last few pieces to me in Roseville, CA

Kathleen recorded the full story behind how she came to own a set of family heirloom china originally purchased by her father in 1958 while in the Navy. She formatted one column of her journaling to wrap in a gentle curve to enhance the shape of the plate. More journaling, printed on vellum, gives an overview of everywhere the china traveled. For an additional graphic element, Kathleen placed a small photo of the china's logo (found on the back of a plate) underneath a page pebble. The watermark effect at the top was created by scanning and manipulating the same logo on the computer.

47 Years…
Kathleen Summers,
Roseville, California
Photo: Jay Dixon Photography,
Livermore, California

Supplies: *Page pebble (Making Memories); cardstocks; vellum; word processing program*

JE T'AIME SENS DESSUS DESSOUS

image

There are many ways to display images for a striking graphic statement. For scrapbookers, the most commonly used image is a photograph. When selecting a photograph to become the focal point of the page, it should be clear and of good quality. The photo should also be impactful—and this is where the fun starts. Creating impact in photography starts with your camera angle. Zoom in for a close-up of a subject's eyes, position yourself high above the subject or photograph details such as a child's muddy shoes. If you don't think about creating impact until after the photo is taken, you can still do so by cropping it into an interesting shape, altering the appearance with image-editing software or simply enlarging it. The number of ways to create "the wow factor" with photos is endless, but it's not the only way to give your pages a graphic-design edge through image. Successful imagery in design can also be created through the repeated use of shapes, lines, patterns and interesting page embellishments. The pages throughout this chapter prove how images can evoke a certain mood, style or energy to grab one's attention without saying a word.

chapter three

Frame an image with smaller circles

1 A circle-cropped focal point draws viewers' attention.

2 An extreme close-up perspective of a face adds uniqueness.

3 Title placement balances circular page elements.

4 Repeated circles create rhythm and energy.

5 Multiple patterns are all in coordinating colors.

6 Strips of coordinating ribbon contrast nicely with the white background, making the focal photo pop.

Your Eyes Are The Windows To Your Soul

Maranatha cropped an enlargement of her son into a circle, then distressed the photo's edges for a strong main image. The dark-background photo pops on white cardstock. Maranatha gave the impactful photo even more emphasis by surrounding it with small patterned paper circles with inked edges. Together, the circles add rhythm and color to the layout.

Your Eyes…
Maranatha Baca, Tulare, California

Supplies: *Patterned paper (KI Memories); metal index tab (7 Gypsies); ribbons (Offray); cardstock; stamping ink*

Circle crop a close-up photo

Jennifer included multiple patterns in this layout but still maintained a graphic feel through the use of circles. Her focal point, title and page accents were all designed this way, creating unity through shape.

Groove is In the Art
Jennifer Lynn Moody, Lewisville, Texas

Supplies: *Patterned papers (KI Memories); textured cardstock (Bazzill); word-processing program (Microsoft Word Art); circle cutter (Fiskars); pen*

Place title inside a circular image

Jessica's title inside a multicolored circle is the perfect complement to a little girl with bubbles. Made of cardstock and patterned paper, it becomes a design element all its own. The direction of the little girl's reach draws one's eye straight to the well-designed title. What's more, the title is also part of a simple quote.

Our Reach…
Jessica Sprague,
Apple Valley, Minnesota

Supplies: *Patterned paper (Treehouse Memories); textured cardstocks (Bazzill); rub-on letters (Heidi Swapp, Making Memories); letter stamps (Making Memories); metal label holder (www.twopeasinabucket.com); stamping ink*

Lisa displayed the concept of growth within a yellow circular image, which also serves as an eye-catching backdrop for her journaling. Photos nestled within the notches around the shape depict the growth of Lisa's son. A similar shape is repeated behind the title to unify the page.

Growth Potential
Lisa Hoel, San Jose, California

Supplies: *Image-editing software (Adobe Photoshop CS); drawing program (Adobe Illustrator CS)*

Enlarged type combined with an interesting shape make this layout very active. Choosing a unique shape to design an entire layout around adds visual depth and motion to any layout. That shape can then be used to enhance any part of the layout, photos, journaling or title.

Focus on a detail shot

Funny how
A simple thing
Like purple wildflowers
Softly waving in the wind
Can make me feel so happy

Janneke drew attention to a single wildflower by cropping it into a circle on the computer. A white border around the flower contrasts with the photo and solid-colored backgrounds, making it stand out more.

Funny How…
Janneke Smit, Agoura, California

Supplies: *Image-editing software (Adobe Photoshop CS); drawing program (CorelDraw 12)*

Draw attention with a star-burst design

The design of a Ferris wheel inspired Oksanna to create an eye-catching star-burst image from cardstock. It also became the backdrop for her title, complete with bottle-cap letters for added dimension. Snapshots were interspersed around the star-burst design, allowing it, rather than a photograph, to take center stage.

To Rock or Not to Rock
Oksanna Pope, Los Gatos, California

Supplies: *Patterned paper, bottle caps, letter stickers (Design Originals); glitter spray, clear beads (Duncan); circle template (Déjà Views); letter stamps (PSX Design); cardstocks; pen; stamping ink*

Theresa used an image of a flower cut from patterned paper to enhance a photo of her daughter. She thought a flower was the perfect image to symbolize beauty, growth and love, which fits nicely with her feelings for her daughter. The positioning of the flower and photograph even makes it look as if the girl is peeking from behind it.

Kärlek
Theresa Lundström, Skelleftea, Sweden

Supplies: *Patterned paper, letter stickers (Basic Grey); chalk ink (Clearsnap); heart punch (EK Success)*

Inspired by an ad in a magazine, Charrie freehand drew random, circular lines on paper and cut them out to form the patterns for her page design. She used the pattern to crop a background design as well as the focal-point photo. It is her creative use of shape and line that success-fully makes the main image more interesting. A silhouette-cropped photo in the corner balances the focal point and lends to the free-spirited look of the design.

Simple Joy
Charrie Shockey, Ardmore, Oklahoma

Supplies: *Letter stickers (American Crafts); rub-on letters (Wordsworth); cardstocks; pen; stamping ink*

Include circles in varying sizes

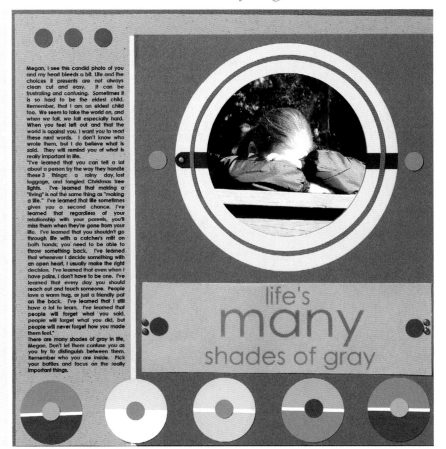

Heide turned to geometric shapes and repetition to showcase a poignant photo of her daughter, who is experi-encing the growing pains of teen years. The circular frame and red ring draw the eye to the photo like a bull's eye on a target, while the linear black mat anchors it. Repeated circles in various sizes—paint samples, punched circles and brads—complement the focal point and add rhythm.

Life's Many Shades of Gray
Heide Lasher, Englewood, Colorado

Supplies: *Textured cardstocks (Bazzill); circle cutter (Creative Memories); mini brads (Making Memories); paint chip samples (from hardware store); vellum*

"On July 16, 1969 more than 30 stories above the launch pad for the huge Saturn V rocket, Neil Armstrong, Buzz Aldrin and Michael Collins walked across this Service Arm from the Launch Tower to the Command Module of Apollo 11. Their next stop: the Moon"

I know the two of you didn't understand what I were so excited about. As far as you could tell, you were just walking through another exhibit. You can call me sentimental, but to me this bright orange walkway represented so much more.

To go to the moon—to put aside the rationality that it could never be done. To see beyond the limits of the possible to a whole new frontier. To imagine, to try, even to fail. But to never give up.

There is nothing more I could pray for you. That you would attempt everything with the idea that failure is not an option. That you would develop a dream and work your hardest to reach it. Know that there will be failures, there will be disappointments, but that you will persevere.

DREAM BIG
reach high

05.21.05

The zigzagging lines of the walkway in this photo allow it to stand alone as a focal point. To break up the strong, straight lines in the photo, Samantha inserted a curved and inked strip of patterned paper. The vertical orientation of the photo also fits with Samantha's "dream big" theme. To allow the photo to be as large as possible, Samantha added her title to the photo with image-editing software.

Dream Big
Samantha Widlund, Minneola, Florida

Supplies: *Patterned paper (Autumn Leaves); image-editing software (Microsoft Picture It!); stamping ink; cardstock*

Silly ... goofy ... funny ... perfect words to describe you two. I love to see you fill your time with silly antics and games. Most of the time it's "Haley-ball" ... Haley makes up the rules and Everett follows ... hilarity ensues. Today ... let's be silly for Mom and her excessive picture taking! Thanks for being good sports. I know you are tired of pictures, but Mom's got to practice!!

The positioning of subjects in a photograph can sometimes be the difference between just a nice photo and a strong focal point. To illustrate Christine's kids' silliness, this photo speaks volumes and is much more representative of the topic than a traditionally posed portrait would be.

Silly
Christine Johnson, Keller, Texas

Supplies: *Letter and parentheses stickers (American Crafts); cardstocks*

Use an image with contrasting light

The bright, contrasting light coming through the airplane window lights up the page and draws attention to the subject. Margie's journaling focuses on her son's interest in the safety manual before takeoff, and the photo clearly captures the moment.

Read, Relax, Travel...
Margie Lundy, Troy, Ohio

Supplies: *Image-editing software (Adobe Photoshop); title design (Tina Chambers, www.digitalscrapbookplace.com)*

This afternoon I was playing with my camera lenses. I was randomly taking pictures of you to test them. We were in my scrapbook room, you were playing with your Matchbox cars. I caught you showing me the winner of the race. This photo speaks volumes to me. Your world revolves around cars. As a toddler, before you could say no more than a dozen words, you would watch cars coming at us, and identify them. "Car, car, truck...." I was amazed at how you could do this. Now at six, you can give more complex informationa bout the cars. Make and model. The little cars are all over the house. In my purse, the floor, in the shower, in your hand. I know where you have been by the trail of cars! I love you, Mommy 1/05

You must always be curious.
— WALT WHITMAN

CAR

97

3

An extreme enlargement of a child's face will give a page a graphic feel all by itself. And with a toy car in hand, the content of this photo also reveals a lot about Judith's son's personality. To complement but not overpower the striking black-and-white image, Judith chose an achromatic color scheme—one with blacks, whites and grays.

Car
Judith Fender, Fletcher,
North Carolina

Supplies: *Patterned papers, letter stickers (Mustard Moon); quote sticker (Autumn Leaves); brads (Karen Foster Design, Office Depot); transparency; cardstocks*

The close-up Sherry took of these daisies, complete with soft focus on some, creates a successful focal point for this page. The white daisy petals contrast nicely with the dark photo background, making them stand out even more. Because the content of the photo is simple, it works to surround it with energetic accents, which also complement the dark photo background well.

Daisy
Sherry Wright, West Branch, Michigan

Supplies: *Patterned paper, ribbon, premade letters and shapes (KI Memories); rickrack (Wrights); distress ink (Ranger); transparency*

My yard consists of thousands of flowers each one unique. But everytime I see a daisy I can not help get a big smile on my face. They are like natures smiling faces Such a cheerful flower they scream happiness and fun. Mother nature must of thought I needed some extra smiles since I did not plant any myself, but somehow hundreds of these happy little guys have appeared and brought a smile to my face!

daisy

I love looking at Ferris Wheels. But don't ask me to get on it. I'm terrified of heights and do not like being stuck on top when people get on it. on the ground. I'm just contempt to watching my kids and husband get on them. This picture was taking on my way back from a meeting. Going there I saw the wheel. but didn't have time to stop. But I made sure to stop by and snap a few pics on my way home!!

Round & Round & Round it goes

The grand curve of the Ferris wheel, in addition to its crisscrossing lines and bright colors, makes it an interesting focal-point image. To balance the strength of the photo, Caroline added bright strips of paper with rounded ends to the other side. Journaling and title were placed to match the shape of the design elements.

Round & Round…
Caroline Huot, Laval, Quebec, Canada

Supplies: *Premade square (KI Memories); textured cardstocks (Bazzill); corner rounder*

Designer's eye

This image is a wonderful example of how an interesting crop can support a layout. Juxtaposed to horizontal color bars, the image creates movement that brings the reader's eyes down to the title. Text added within the space of the horizontal bars completes the sophistication of this page.

Moments

.natural
.filled with joy

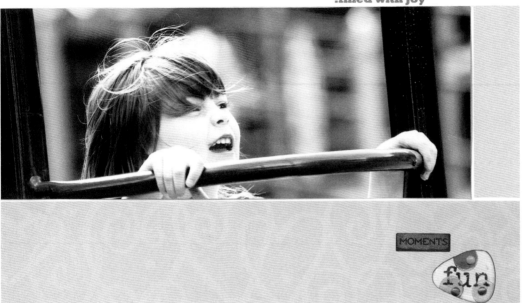

The joy in a single childhood moment is captured on Christine's daughter's face. She kept the page clean by using simple embellishments and mostly neutral tones to keep the focus on the photograph. The horizontal orientation helps create an eye-catching image.

Moments
Christine Traversa, Joliet, Illinois

Supplies: *Patterned paper, stickers (All My Memories); cardstock*

MOMENTS

fun

It's hard to deny the impression an image creates when it extends edge to edge, forming the entire background of a page. The vast expanse of the water provides lots of space for other page elements. Using page-design software, Kathy placed journaling, additional photos and a title over her focal image. Thin white borders around the smaller photos help them to stand out on the background.

Reverie
Kathy Altaras, Addison, Texas

Supplies: *Image-editing software (Microsoft Publisher with Digital Image Pro)*

Sometimes it's easy to forget how much you have on your shoulders. After a day spent chasing after Sophie, I am often envious that you spent your day in the "civilized world". Envious that you had lunch in a restaurant and didn't have to worry about cleaning food up off the floor. Envious that you went for coffee mid afternoon without lugging anyone in and out of a carseat. Envious that you got to use the restroom by yourself!

During those times I often forget that you worry on a daily basis about the mortgage, Sophie's college fund, our future. I forget that there is an immense amount of stress involved with being the sole breadwinner for our family. I forget that you do the laundry, help with the household chores, maintain the cars, pay the bills, mow the lawn, take the garbage out and do a myriad of things in the ebb and flow of our daily lives.

And, aside from all you do, you go to work in an incredibly hectic, frenzied and stressful environment every day. Making enormous decisions for the future of a company that you care about. You often don't have time to eat lunch because there are too many phone calls to make. Your afternoon coffee break may be the first time you've stepped away from your desk all day.

You have the weight of the world on your shoulders. I will try to do a better job of remembering that. I love you honey.

An extreme enlargement of her husband's face coupled with a map to simulate the world creates a dynamic focal point on Lisa's spread. The inward-facing photograph draws one into the spread to focus on the journaling and other details Lisa included.

Weight of the World
Lisa VanderVeen, Mendham, New Jersey

Supplies: *Epoxy letter stickers (Creative Imaginations); textured cardstocks (Bazzill); letter brads, decorative brads, label holder (Queen & Co.); map*

Through your eyes,
I see myself,
only better.

love, mommy

When Missy first saw this photo she took of her son, the reflection in his sunglasses caught her attention. With a little help from image-editing software, she let the glasses take center stage on this page. On the computer, she layered a black-and-white copy of the photograph over a color copy, then used the erase tool to allow the color of the sunglasses to shine through.

Through Your Eyes...
Missy Sauter, Houston, Texas

Supplies: *Patterned paper (Chatterbox); textured cardstocks (Prism Papers); rub-on letters, chipboard square letters (Making Memories); ribbon (Perfect Ribbon Co.)*

Build a layout around image color

For a dramatic photo effect, Missy turned the rest of her photo black-and-white while leaving the flower in color. The focus on the flower is also the concept mentioned in her journaling. Missy selected layout colors based on the flower.

A Moment Like This
Missy Gerace, Manchester, Connecticut

Supplies: *Image-editing software (Jasc Paint Shop Pro)*

a MOMENT like this...

Erin, you have a talent for finding all the prettiest flowers in our garden. When you picked this prefect pink daisy and you held it up to your face, it struck me. You are growing up faster than I can imagine, but thankfully you do still go slow enough sometimes to stop and smell the flowers. It is moments like this that I love to stop and watch you bloom and grow...

(June 2005)

Superimpose an image

bringing
it on
home
for the
last game
of his
first **t-ball**
SeaSon

July 15, 2005

matthew

With image-editing software, Ronnie added a picture of her son's face to the sky above the baseball field to make it appear as if Matthew was looking back on his last T-ball season. The face image gives color to the light sky and balances Ronnie's journaling on the left side. In addition, Ronnie positioned the face looking inward so viewer's eyes are led onto the page and not away from it.

T-Ball Season
Ronnie McCray, St. James, Missouri

Supplies: *Image-editing software (Adobe Photoshop Elements 2.0); digital letters (Rebecca Rios, Computer Scrapping Elements 2 Yahoo Group)*

Model an image after a poster

Judith paid tribute to her husband on a uniquely simple page that she modeled after a poster for the Academy Awards. To create an Oscarlike image featuring her husband, she used image-editing software to lighten the image, increase the contrast and apply a cutout filter. Then she silhouette-cut the image and adhered it to four solid cardstock blocks. She lightly chalked the background to give it more dimension.

Hubby
Judith Mara, Lancaster, Massachusetts

Supplies: *Image-editing software (Adobe Photoshop Elements 3.0); letter sticker (EK Success); brad; chalk; cardstocks*

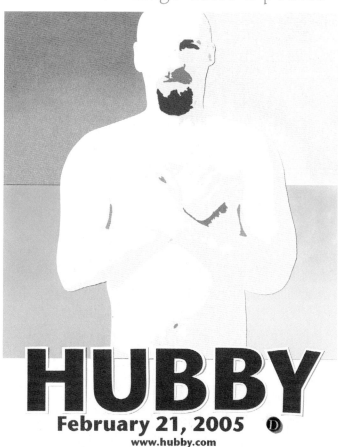

HUBBY
February 21, 2005
www.hubby.com

Rather than using a traditional mother-and-son portrait, Ann chose a more interesting silhouette. Offset by the bright lights of the tree, this page is simple yet communicates her message without being so literal in direction.

Add mystery with a silhouette

On this Christmas page, Ann reflects on how she can truly relate to the miracle birth of the holiday after having her own son. She chose a silhouette photo of herself and her son looking at the Christmas tree to illustrate her thoughts. Over the brightly lit tree, the dark silhouettes stand out in contrast.

Comfort & Joy
Ann Hetzel Gunkel, Chicago, Illinois
Photo: David J. Gunkel, Chicago, Illinois

Supplies: *Image-editing software (Adobe Photoshop 7.0); digital papers, tab, tag, and transparency (Design Butcher, Grade A Scraps Vol. 2, www.scrapgirl.com)*

The Many Faces of

Jennifer combined four photos of her daughter's many expressions for this page, but enlarged her favorite for emphasis. The vibrancy found in her photos, including her daughter's bright pink shirt, made it unnecessary to add other embellishments. The images successfully capture Katelyn's personality with nothing more than a white background and black type.

The Many Faces of You
Jennifer Wilmarth,
Ypsilanti, Michigan

Supplies: *Cardstock*

Katelyn, you have so many funny expressions. If anyone wanted to know what you were thinking all they would have to do is look at your wonderful face. You can be so many things in the space of a minute. You have always been that way. I love to take pictures of you because I am never sure what will show up on the print. You always surprise me. You are my silly, wonderful, sarcastic, beautiful girl. You keep life interesting. Don't ever change. 08.07.05

Highlight a single element with color

Free Spirit

Pink and strong. Who says a girl wearing *Pink* can't beat 20 boys in a little muttin bustin' competition. You go girl, wear that *Pink* color strong.

Angela wanted this layout to reflect her daughter's tomboy image while incorporating the fact that she is a girl and loves pink. She balanced the context of her focal-point image, a rodeo, by turning the photo black-and-white and leaving her daughter's shirt pink. This choice makes her daughter pop on the gray background and achieves Angela's tomboy/girly layout concept.

Free Spirit
Angela Svoboda, Ord, Nebraska

Supplies: *Image-editing software (Adobe Photoshop CS2); digital papers, tag, and ribbon (Scraps of Fun CD- All Girls, www.ditigalscrapbookplace.com); digital stitching (www.computerscrapbookdesigns.com)*

Add shapes that mimic those in a photo

A pattern of circles in different colors and sizes unifies Rebecca's page. The design mimics the content of her photo—pots and pans spread across her kitchen floor. The repeated circles that bleed off the edges of the page also offer the feeling of movement and energy, much like a young boy and his makeshift drum set.

Music Maker
Rebecca Lehn-Hilliard,
Milwaukee, Wisconsin

Supplies: *Textured cardstocks (Bazzill); ribbon (Michaels); letter sticker (Imagination Project); circle-cutting system (Creative Memories); circle punch (EK Success); colored staples (Making Memories)*

December 14, 2004

Music Maker

You really need a set of drums, Jalen. You love to take out all my pots and pans, spoons, spatulas, anything that will make noise so you can POUND and BANG. I love that you enjoy making music so much but my ears and my pots are taking a beating. I'm glad you told Daddy and I that you want a set of real drums for Christmas next year. Maybe then I won't have to trip over dishes in the middle of the kitchen floor!

Turn a photo upside down

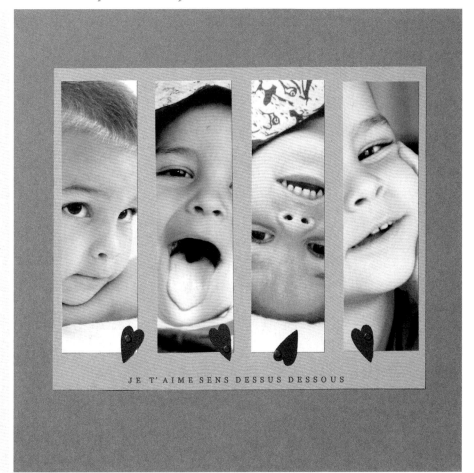

JE T'AIME SENS DESSUS DESSOUS

Sometimes multiple images placed next to each other can form a single focal point. Severine's tightly cropped vertical photos of her son do just that. She achieved variation throughout her repeated pattern of photos by turning one shot upside down and leaving it in color. A single, simple statement, "I Love You Upside Down," fits perfectly with her design.

Je T'aime Sens Dessus Dessous
Severine Di Giacomo, Cugy, Vaud, Switzerland

Supplies: *Textured cardstocks (Bazzill); mini brads (Junkitz); heart punch (Marvy)*

Close-up photos of ornaments placed next to each other form single focal points for each side of this spread. On black backgrounds with thin mats of red, the lighter, sparkling detail shots show up well. To enhance the images, Emma filled title letters with a section of out-of-focus background taken from one of the photos.

Christmas Glass
Emma Finlay, Sutton, Dublin, Ireland

Supplies: *Image-editing software (Adobe Photoshop 5.0)*

Heather had a much different layout in mind before she printed these photos of her sister. When these four shots came out of the printer together, she thought they made a stronger focal point as one unit. She designed the rest of the layout around them, including wrapping her journaling around the four photos.

Technicolor Sissy
Heather McHarg, Agoura Hills, California

Supplies: *Patterned paper (Basic Grey); rub-on letters (Making Memories); ribbon (Offray); stamping ink; pen; staples; cardstock*

Crop photos and accents to the same size and shape

A pattern of multiple squares was a good design choice for Laura's photos that were taken at a distance. No single photo creates a focal point, but the combination of small squares comes together for a rhythmic layout. Inked edges of cardstock squares and eyelets add dimension to the page. Shots of her daughter in action, each slightly different, create a sense of movement.

Determination
Laura O'Donnell,
West Chester, Pennsylvania

Supplies: *Patterned papers (Creative Imaginations, Sweetwater); textured cardstocks (Bazzill); letter stamps (Ma Vinci's Reliquary); distress ink (Ranger); eyelets; pen*

A single photo of a tiny shoe is precious, but it's the grouping of cardstock squares at the top of the page that captures one's attention. Squares in green, gold, rust, brown and aqua lend somewhat of a retro feel that complements the shoe style. Edges inked in dark brown provide added contrast to the white background. A title stamped in colors similar to some of the squares pulls everything together.

First Shoes
Jennifer Harrison, Orem, Utah

Supplies: *Patterned paper (KI Memories); textured cardstocks (Bazzill); ribbon (Provo Craft); letter stamps (Hero Arts); stamping inks*

Cut circles from different patterns

Circles of patterned paper in coordinating shades come together to create impact on this simple page. The placement of the circles makes it seem like they could roll right off the page—a clever design choice for a roly-poly bugs layout. Because it's hard to see the bugs themselves, the playful circles add interest. One even serves as a canvas for journaling.

Polies
Samantha Widlund, Minneola, Florida

Supplies: *Patterned papers (KI Memories); textured cardstocks (Bazzill); chipboard letters (Heidi Swapp); photo corners (3L); acrylic paint; pen*

This unique patterned paper design helps draw attention to Desiree's smaller, sepia-toned photo. And with a significant amount of open space on either end of the focal point, one's eye automatically goes to the center of the page where the action is.

Lucky
Desiree McClellan, Wichita, Kansas

Supplies: *Patterned paper, metal word accent (American Crafts); cardstocks*

A single vertical photo on a horizontal striped background makes the photo of Kim's husband stand out on this page. The subtle background shades match those in the picture, setting a calm tone. A digital shadow placed behind the photo makes it stand out from the background even more.

I Love This Man
Kim Carey, Muskegon, Michigan

Supplies: *Digital papers (www.scrapbook-bytes .com); image-editing software (Microsoft Digital Image Suite Editor)*

i love this man

this is the man i prayed for, this is the man who prayed for me. in him i know i am never alone, in him i honor God, with him i worship God. he makes me laugh even when i think i'd rather be sad. he makes me feel safe even from the past. he brings me joy, he accepts me, he will always love me, this i know. he is thoughtful, caring, loving, considerate, intelligent, brave, a true man. he is never rash, he let's me be free, he is my best friend, he is my love, he is my future, he is my past, he is my all.

this is my husband

20 YEARS from now, you will be more disappointed by the things you didn't do than the things you did do. So, throw off the bowlines. Sail away from the safe harbor. Catch the trade winds in your sails. EXPLORE, DREAM, DISCOVER.

Mark Twain

A downloaded graphic image that was repeated gives this page a cohesive feel. In simple black, the images do not overpower the photo but make the page more interesting to look at thanks to the use of other shapes. They also help balance the weight created by the dark photo background. The quote Amber chose also stands out more due to the images that surround it

20 Years
Amber Clark, Greenville, Ohio

Supplies: *Graphic image dingbat (downloaded from Internet); textured cardstock (Bazzill)*

Designer's eye

This layout achieves visual balance by including text and graphics on the right in the same space the photo covers on the left. This visual-balance principle can be repeated in any layout by applying the same placement technique.

Insert photos in an unusual pattern

Photos cropped into unusual shapes and connected by interesting lines set this page apart. While experimenting with a paint program, Adine had altered a photo of her son using a "fishbowl" effect and wanted a mat to go with it. The shapes in this premade paper design fit perfectly. They accentuate the odd qualities of "Frog Boy" that Adine describes in her journaling. Furthermore, the design provides the letter "O" in "boy" for her title.

Frog Boy
Adine Moynihan, Manchester, Connecticut

Supplies: *Patterned paper (Lazar Studiowerx); acrylic letters (KI Memories); image-editing program (Jasc Paint Shop Pro); pens; stamping ink; cardstock*

Add stripes to fit an era

Angela gave her somewhat faded, older photograph a boost by pairing it with stripes that fit the era. Patterned paper and cardstock strips that coordinate perfectly with the colors in the photo bring this page alive. The stripes are also very similar to a boy's shirt in the photo.

Retro Campers
Angela Biggley, Windsor, Ontario, Canada

Supplies: *Patterned paper (Chatterbox); textured cardstocks (Bazzill); acrylic sticker (KI Memories)*

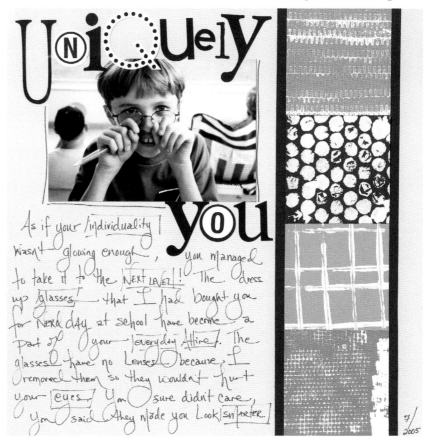

Rachel couples her son's unique-ness with an original, hand-stamped image. She stamped toy car-wheels, bubble wrap and mesh into acrylic paint and applied them to cardstock for added shapes and texture. Rachel proves that stamped creations can work well on graphic-style pages and give them that little something extra.

Uniquely You
Rachel Ellington, Logansport, Indiana

Supplies: *Letter stickers (American Crafts, Doodle-bug Design); textured cardstocks (Bazzill); acrylic paint; pen; found objects for stamping*

Let an image speak for itself

Kristie loved this moment between her son and his grandma, but the original photo contained distracting colors. She turned the photo black-and-white to keep the viewer's attention on this special shared moment. Little else is needed to enhance the spirit of love that the photo reveals.

Nanna Love
Kristie David, Houston, Texas

Supplies: *Image-editing software (Adobe Photoshop); type brushes (www.misprintedtype.com)*

Storebror och Lillasyster

Att få vara stor, viktig och omhändertagande.
Att få vara förebild och bästa kompis.
Att alltid finnas där med en hjälpande hand -
det är att vara storebror.
Att få vara liten, betydelsefull och
omhändertagen.
Att ha någon att se upp till och alltid ha en bästa
vän till hands.
Att få ta en trygg hand och bli ledd genom livet -
det är att vara lillasyster.

Translated "Big Brother, Little Sister," this page captures the sweet moment when Malena's son took his sister's hand and walked with her. Since the photo is not enlarged, enclosing it in an interesting shape helps draw attention to it. Malena also chose light shades for her layout to contrast with the darker hues of the photo, allowing the photo to stand out even more.

Storebror och Lillasyster
Malena Andersson,
Hallestad, Sweden

Supplies: *Patterned papers (American Traditional Designs, Sweetwater); decorative brads (Making Memories); leaf punch (Punch Bunch); silk flowers; thread; cardstock*

Those Playful Eyes

fun

play

Your playful nature is so evident in your big blue eyes! I love to see your smiles and listen to your jokes. I love the funny You I see!

Holly, Feb 05

In this computer-generated layout, Teri-Lynn kept the focus on her daughter's eyes by adding a translucent layer resembling vellum in a curved shape. The curve makes it look as though Holly is peering from behind the "vellum." Furthermore, because Teri-Lynn's photo was slightly blurry, the translucent layer minimizes this effect.

Those Playful Eyes
Teri-Lynn Masters, Truro,
Nova Scotia, Canada

Supplies: *Image-editing software (Jasc Paint Shop Pro); digital papers and accents (Staci Schall)*

Place photos along a curve

A curved line extending the length of three photos helps bring them together to create a single focal point. Tightly cropped to focus on her daughter's eyes, Jessica's photos are stronger as a unit than if spread in random fashion over the entire background. The design with ample open space clearly captures a single moment of discovery that Jessica intended.

Bah-ten
Jessica Sprague, Apple Valley, Minnesota

Supplies: *Patterned paper (My Mind's Eye); textured cardstock (Bazzill)*

'BAH-ten'

Rowen discovers the shutter release.
08.08.05

Color is a very impactful element. By transforming her main image to yellow-orange, a warm hue, Lisa captures the idea of hot and sunny summer days. Her color choice is also subtle and allows her message to communicate.

Incorporate a pattern of dots

memories
of summer

- making slip and slides out of plastic tarps and the garden hose

- frozen otter pops and sucking the last little bit of juice out of the plastic wrapper

- having picnics in the backyard under the apricot tree

- running around barefoot

- talking into the fan because it made my voice all weird

- going camping at Lake San Antonio and water skiing

- getting a tan line on my feet from my flip-flops

- squishing around in mud holes we would dig out in back of the house

- getting new school clothes and a new binder with supplies

august

With image-editing software, Lisa created a dot pattern around the edges of the photo that gets smaller and lighter as it reaches her journaling. The pattern seems to radiate out slowly, much like the sun's rays or a breeze from a fan. The fan facing toward the journaling helps draw viewers into Lisa's text.

August
Lisa Hoel, San Jose, California

Supplies: *Image-editing software (Adobe Photoshop CS); drawing program (Adobe Illustrator CS)*

A curved line along one edge of Sharon's focal photo lends a sense of movement and supports the idea of a basketball curving toward the basket. She placed her title along the curved edge to emphasize it further.

Jump...Higher
Sharon Maughan, Salem, Virginia

Supplies: *Image-editing software (Adobe Photoshop Elements 3.0); ribbon (Signature Kit, www .shabbyprincess.com); date stamp (Katie Pertiet, www .designerdigitals.com); paper (artist's own design)*

Spring in Virginia came as a wonderful surprise! February and March brought warm weather and beautiful blue skies and the kids were able to spend lots of time outside. Craig spent the nice weather practicing his 'shots'. The new **BASKETBALL** hoop could be lowered for him, but NO.... he wanted it ALL the way up!! He made most of his shots at this height, much to our surprise and his delight!

CRAIG
03.12.05

Mimic baseball stitching in design

2005 State Pitch, Hit & Run
9 & 10 YEAR OLD DIVISION
Cole Svoboda
3RD PLACE

Stitching designed to resemble a baseball through the center of this page supports Angela's theme. The curved line further complements the theme. In the top left corner, the curve helps draw attention to the photo of her son.

Pitch Hit Run
Angela Svoboda, Ord, Nebraska

Supplies: *Image-editing software (Adobe Photoshop CS2); digital papers and accents (Angie Svoboda, www.computer scrapbookdesigns.com)*

P You're getting big, Pete. It's funny though, I thought that I would be sad that you're getting older but I'm not. I love being able to talk to you and carry on a decent conversation. I'm excited to see what kind of interest you'll have as you get older. Will they change or will they stay the same? Don't get me wrong- I'm not in the least bit hurrying you to grow up. I'm a bit nervous about you going to Sunday school in September and I'll cherish your last year at home with me but we can't deny that you're getting big; and I think that I'm OK with that. ■ ■ ■

HE'S ...BiG

GETTING

layout

Graphic designers look at the elements they have and work creatively to select the best possible arrangement for them. When all the text and images come together in a cohesive way that communicates well, the layout is a success. In the end, the types of layout they choose will determine how impactful their designs are. Similarly, readers of your scrapbooks should be able to pause and enjoy the message you are trying to convey without it being too complicated or cluttered. In many cases, one photo, a single-word title and a succinct sentence are all that is needed to create an effective layout. On the other hand, multiple photos in different sizes, more detailed journaling and even a few embellishments create the best layout in other cases. The artists in this chapter used the space they had efficiently to come up with the best possible arrangement of page elements.

why it works:
layout

Enhance photos with color blocks

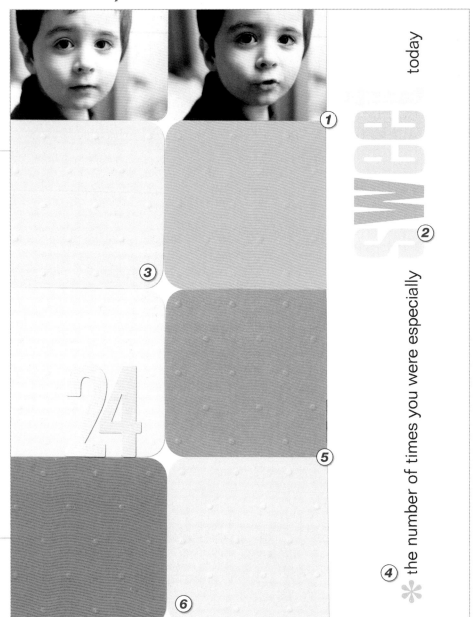

1 Space is utilized efficiently with a balanced mix of minimal journaling, photos, design elements and a title.

2 Multicolored letters pull readers into the journaling.

3 Cardstock color blocks unify the design and pull the reader's eyes from the photos down to the numeric title.

4 Placement of vertical journaling balances the black-and-white photos.

5 Designing the page on a vertical grid gives organization to page elements.

6 Repeated use of color creates rhythm.

For a unique spin on appreciating a child's good behavior, Desiree titled this page with the number of times her son was sweet in one day. One's eye is drawn to the colorful pattern of squares, topped with the most important component—pictures of her son. The word "sweet" created in the same colors as the squares becomes a design element all its own and helps balance the page.

24
Desiree McClellan, Wichita, Kansas

Supplies: *Metal numbers (KI Memories); rub-on symbol (K & Company); embossed stationery (source unknown); cardstock*

Choose a focal point from a series

That Look...

Anna Beth, you have two expressions that have gotten a lot of attention lately. One is your darling smile. The other is what we lovingly call "that look." In fact, we often call it "The Bob Look" because it's the same frown your dad makes when he is analyzing or concentrating on something. Strangers everywhere from the grocery store to the doctor's office have remarked on your piercing stare and furrowed brow. "Is she angry?" they ask. "She must not like strangers." They don't realize that you are actually quite friendly and jovial. Genetics simply take over when you encounter a situation that needs to be analyzed. Just be careful using that frown on your daddy, though. He's sure to say,

"Don't give me that look, I invented that look!"

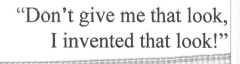

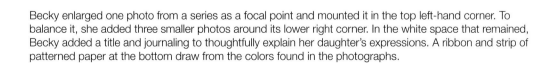

Becky enlarged one photo from a series as a focal point and mounted it in the top left-hand corner. To balance it, she added three smaller photos around its lower right corner. In the white space that remained, Becky added a title and journaling to thoughtfully explain her daughter's expressions. A ribbon and strip of patterned paper at the bottom draw from the colors found in the photographs.

That Look
Becky Mercer, Newark, Delaware

Supplies: *Patterned paper (Rusty Pickle); ribbon (Offray); cardstock*

SPRING '05

Slides can be scary, but only at first!

It takes two to teeter-totter!

It's funner to play with a frined.

Mom worries and dad ...
well, dad doesn't!

Sometimes you need a little lift
to get up into a swing.

There's the big kids playground,
and the little kids playground.
Things are always funner at the
BIG kids playground

Sometimes you fall, but if you
jump up and brush off,
you're usually OK!

It's never fun to leave
when you're having a great time.

Primary PRINCIPLES
you can learn at the park.

Angela uses a literal design translation of primary colors to reinforce her page theme of "primary principles." The computer-generated scrapbook page includes a combination of three duotone photographs (each primary color + black) in vertical stripes as a focal point. Other page elements in the same primary colors create harmony, while a solid black title drives home the entire theme of the layout.

Primary Principles
Angela Barton, Hyrum, Utah

Supplies: *Image-editing software (Adobe Photoshop CS2)*

Designer's eye

Concept can be communicated on many different levels. Angela chose a literal translation by using primary colors to support her content. Layout, typeface, word play and shape can all be used to enhance your concept within a layout.

Equal parts of circles, photos and journaling create a pleasing marriage of text and images on Kim's page. Patterned strips along the top and bottom balance the page. Circular letter stickers were placed directly over the dots on the paper so they mesh perfectly with the design element.

Discover Lillian
Kim Musgrove, Lewiston, New York

Supplies: *Patterned paper (Daisy D's); letter stickers (Li'l Davis Designs); cardstock*

discover

almost two and i'm finally discovering what you're all about. you see, you are quite different. you came into this world being a fighter and strong-willed and only now do i realize that that is how you are going to be in life. you always fight for what is rightfully yours, not letting your big sis get the better of you. if you get hurt, it doesn't take long for you to move on and forget your pain. i know you will overcome any obstacles set in front of you. stay strong little girl and always fight for what you believe in. i love you Lillian.

l i l l i a n

Position title to fit layout

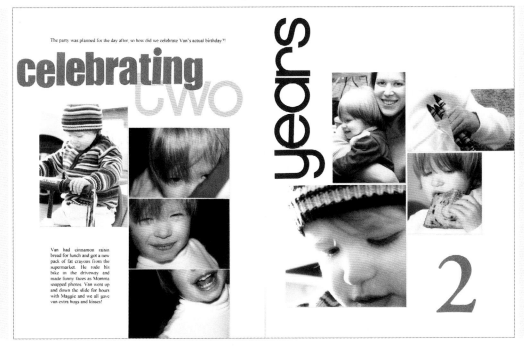

The party was planned for the day after, so how did we celebrate Van's actual birthday?!

celebrating two

years

Van had cinnamon raisin bread for lunch and got a new pack of fat crayons from the supermarket. He rode his bike in the driveway and made funny faces as Momma snapped photos Van went up and down the slide for hours with Maggie and we all gave van extra hugs and kisses!

2

Jennifer balanced her cropped photos with journaling printed on a clean white canvas. Carefully positioned letter stickers span the spread horizontally and vertically, using white space efficiently without stealing any attention from the photographs. She included a color from her subject's hat in the title. The arrangement of the photos adds rhythm to the spread.

Celebrating Two Years
Jennifer Harrison, Orem, Utah

Supplies: *Letter and number stickers (American Crafts, SEI); cardstock*

Format journaling columns to match layout

I am a self-proclaimed nag. Yes, yes…your dear wife…a nag—I admit it! I try hard some days to just hush and let everyone be, but that inner voice gets the best of me sometimes and I instinctively just run my mouth.

Looking over photos today I remember what a good sport you were being while I tried to test the setting of my camera. I know you hate to have your photo taken and I know you hate to be nagged, but you are so good to me…you just wait it out.

[jj - photo taken july 26, 2004]
Your demeanor is classic. You never shout, and you don't argue. Sure you voice your unwillingness to participate in certain things and yet sometimes you will do them anyway…like stand still and let me snap picture after picture! You let things roll off your back with an acceptance and love that seems to come so easy for you.

On my side of the family I am the easy-going, 'que sera sera' person, but between the two of us I could feel pretty neurotic and shameful some days! The way you handle life and people has influenced me greatly over the years, though. I am able to deal with things in a much more calm and clear manner. I am less argumentative, less worrisome about the little things and yes, even less of a nag!

Jennifer's layout records what she appreciates about her husband's personality and admits a flaw of her own at the same time. She formatted the journaling columns on each side to correspond with the orientation of the photos and paper squares. The placement of the journaling on either side balances the spread. Cool blue open space sets a quiet, pensive mood.

Your Demeanor...
Jennifer Harrison, Orem, Utah

Supplies: *Patterned papers (Basic Grey, Chatterbox, KI Memories, My Mind's Eye, SEI); flower stamp (Close To My Heart); chick stamp (Savvy Stamps); square punch (EK Success); stamping ink; cardstocks*

Piece together a photo montage

Heidi designed a photo montage to document her daughter's 18-month birthday. Using the colors in the leg warmers as inspiration, she chose photos with colored backgrounds of the same value (the lightness or darkness of a color). The pastel shades come together to make a well-coordinated page.

Lexi
Heidi Herrod, Winnipeg,
Manitoba, Canada
Photos: Gingersnaps, Winnipeg,
Manitoba, Canada

Supplies: *Image-editing software (Adobe Photoshop 7.0)*

Include detail shots at different angles

To help document her love for shoes, Melissa utilizes an age-old ploy of the advertising industry to draw in the viewer's eye—detail shots. These close-ups show her shoes from every angle, making it look as if one could reach out and try them on. Matting the images on black cardstock creates contrast from the white background, allowing them to stand out even more.

Shoe Fetish
Melissa Godin, Lorne,
New Brunswick, Canada

Supplies: *Textured cardstocks (Bazzill); ribbon, letter stickers (American Crafts); rub-on letters (KI Memories); rub-on words (Doodlebug Design); metal-rimmed vellum tag (Making Memories)*

Shoes!! Who doesn't love shoes? The style, the variety, what is not to love. I'm a tad bit obsessed with them. I want to own a million pairs. My budget won't allow that, but when I see a great shoe at a great price I have to pick them up. These are my latest obsession. The rounded toe, plaid fabric, high heel, cute little bow. They were too hip, and trendy to just sit there on the shelf. I HAD to buy them. Right? Some people might say I have too many shoes, and I say there is not such thing. I wouldn't have to go far to find lots of ladies who agree with that statement. My mom for example is shoe crazy just like me. I'm so happy she passed along her shopping gene. My best friend Jana, also a shoe lover. I Think she is a tad more obsessed than I. Her last shopping trip resulted in four pairs of shoes!! Oh, the joy. My secret wish is to get sent on TLC's 'what not to wear' and spend my whole 5,000$ on shoes! Just like Stacey's, she has wicked shoes. Mmmmmmm. Shoe heaven.

Choose patterned paper to match the subject

When Vickie's daughter came home from circus day at preschool with her face painted, she remembered an energetic patterned paper that would match her daughter's face perfectly. In addition, a bright orange background, whimsical flower embellishments and a fun stamped and embossed title complement a 4-year-old's energy. Smaller photos framed in white wrap around the lower left corner of the focal photo, while the title wraps around the upper right corner to balance the layout.

4 Weeks Into 4
Vickie Brown, Livingston, Tennessee

Supplies: *Patterned paper (Scenic Route Paper Co.); textured cardstocks (Bazzill); letter and asterisk stamps (MoBe' Stamps!); mini brads (Lasting Impressions); stamping ink; embossing powder; pen*

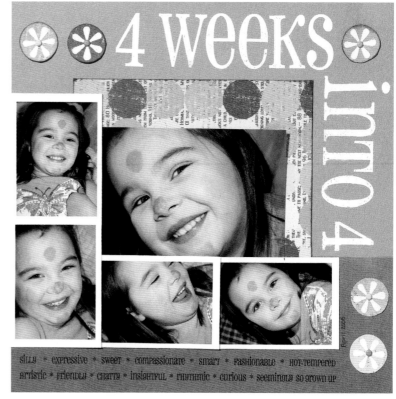

Stage shots for added impact

Amanda wanted to remember her son's clever way of describing yesterday, so she used it as her page title. She staged a few shots of Noah standing at the calendar in order to illustrate his phrase and added journaling that describes how he came up with it. She added a filter to her photos for an interesting effect and chose secondary colors—purple, green and orange—to enhance them on a spread.

The Day Behind Last Night
Amanda N. Probst, Fort Collins, Colorado

Supplies: *Letter stamps (Making Memories); textured cardstocks (Bazzill); corner rounder (EK Success); acrylic paint*

A dramatic detail shot of a drop of rain on a table ledge creates an interesting perspective for Janet's page. Rhythm is achieved through the repetition of small foam squares, which also adds dimension and texture to the page. Small rhinestones embedded in several squares support the drop of rain concept. Extending her title over the photo and cardstock beside it pulls the layout together.

A Drop of Rain
Janet Ohlson, Plainfield, Illinois

Supplies: *Foam squares (Creative Imaginations); rub-on letters, rhinestones (Heidi Swapp); cardstock*

It seems pretty insignificant. But in the middle of one of the worst droughts on record, it can mean a lot to a lot of people.
July 2005

a drop of rain...

Model after a travel brochure

To maximize the amount of space she had for pictures, Christine wrapped smaller photos around the larger ones, a technique she's often seen in travel brochures. While packed with information and interesting images, the page still conveys a clean, graphic feel. She added word plaques and a rub-on title directly over her focal photos to further draw the eye to her favorite shots.

England
Christine Stoneman, Cumberland, Ontario, Canada

Supplies: *Patterned paper (Club Scrap); rub-on letters, decorative brads, label holder, word plaques (Making Memories); distress and walnut ink (Ranger); cardstock*

Design an accent based on art

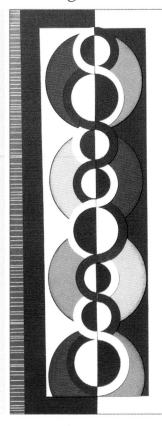

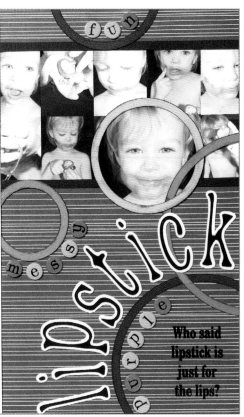

Amber's page has fun elements from edge to edge, yet still maintains a neat, graphic appearance. Inspired by a piece of art she found online, Amber's intricate circle design adds rhythm to the page. Other circles in various areas of the page unify the layout and add even more energy. She created variation within a repeated pattern by enlarging and circle-cropping one photo in a series of small square shots. The interwoven black and white of her circular design is carried through to her title letters, unifying the layout further. Finally, purple letter brads give the page dimension.

Lipstick
Amber Baley, Waupun, Wisconsin

Supplies: *Patterned paper (KI Memories); textured cardstocks (Bazzill); letter brads (Queen & Co.); letter stickers (Mustard Moon); circle cutter (Creative Memories); transparency; stamping ink*

Unify a design with color

Bright colors sprinkled and repeated across this page unify the design. Circles repeated on the initial capital letter, in the corner of the focal photo and along the bottom in black also bring the design together. With black-and-white photos, red, blue and chartreuse accents add life to the page.

Hockey Is Life
Rebecca Saunders,
Yarmouth Port, Massachusetts

Supplies: *Image-editing software (Adobe Photoshop CS)*

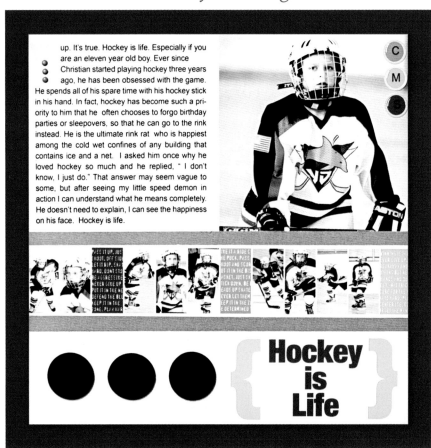

Jennifer's photos are energetic and create a lot of weight on the left side, but the layout is balanced due to the vibrant title and texture of the flower accent. A strip of playful patterned paper running the width of the page further balances the design.

Funny You
Jennifer Harrison, Orem, Utah

Supplies: *Patterned paper (Li'l Davis Designs); letter stickers (Doodlebug Design, SEI); cardstock; silk flower; brad*

An asymmetrical layout is engaging and dynamic. It can be challenging to find a good balance with your page elements, but the layout will be much stronger in the end. Color, typeface and embellishments can all help support the weight that images convey in design.

The White House

"The House that is White"

05 25 05

To showcase a photo of the White House, Kim appropriately chose patriotic red, white and blue accents for this digital layout. A half circle containing her journaling balances a circular "DC" accent in the upper left-hand corner. Tiny circles along the top and bottom add a symmetrical element to the page. On the dark green lawn in the photo, white type contrasts nicely and coordinates with the White House.

The White House
Kim Mauch, Portland, Oregon

Supplies: *Digital papers and accents (Kristie, www.theshabbyshoppe.com); letter brushes (Rebecca Digrazzio, www.scrapbookbytes.com)*

Highlight a collection with repetition

rarities

JJ and I have been collecting Sublime memorabilia since before we met. It's actually the reason why we met, so our collection is a big part of our family. We worked together tracking down items. We made connections with people from record companies and even guys in the band!

Getting a tip on a record or some miscellaneous band-related item was such a rush! We had a list of contacts to check in with regularly and all of the record store guys were so good to us! I remember the day I called this little shop in San Diego and the owner told me he had just gotten back from a sidewalk sale where he found the beer bottle and sardine can for me! I paid over the phone and called JJ right away to tell him about our score!

These two items were handmade by the band, so they became priceless items we held dear over the years. Our lives shifted from collectors long ago, but we have proudly held onto and displayed our Sublime rarities. Recently, we decided it was kind of silly to hold onto certain things when we could still get some good money for them. It felt like time to pass them onto the next die-hard fan to display and admire.

40oz beer & Badfish co. sardines 1998-2005

To represent her and her husband's collection of Sublime memorabilia, named after the band, Jennifer took detail shots of two prized finds in the collection. Repeated photos of the can and bottle taken at slightly different angles creates rhythm. Lots of open space keeps one's eye on the details of these items, which clearly shows their importance in the collection.

Collect
Jennifer Harrison, Orem, Utah

Supplies: *Letter stickers (American Crafts); rub-on letters (Autumn Leaves); cardstock*

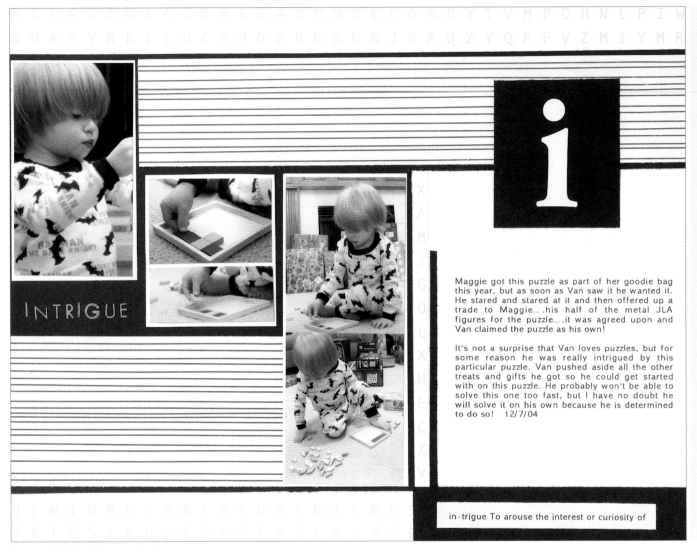

INTRIGUE

Maggie got this puzzle as part of her goodie bag this year, but as soon as Van saw it he wanted it. He stared and stared at it and then offered up a trade to Maggie....his half of the metal JLA figures for the puzzle....it was agreed upon and Van claimed the puzzle as his own!

It's not a surprise that Van loves puzzles, but for some reason he was really intrigued by this particular puzzle. Van pushed aside all the other treats and gifts he got so he could get started with on this puzzle. He probably won't be able to solve this one too fast, but I have no doubt he will solve it on his own because he is determined to do so!   12/7/04

in·trigue To arouse the interest or curiosity of

Jennifer captured her son's fascination with a puzzle by using "word search" patterned paper. Blocks of black cardstock are strategically placed behind photos, an initial and a definition to balance the page. Color choices mimic those in her son's pajamas.

Intrigue
Jennifer Harrison, Orem, Utah

Supplies: *Patterned papers (KI Memories); letter sticker (American Crafts); letter stamps (Close To My Heart); stamping ink; cardstocks*

EXplOrinG

8

MonThs

pull

Noah,
At 8 months, you were getting so
inquisitive. The world around you was just
fascinating. Dad and I loved to watch you
looking at yourself in the mirror. You
always gave a big, gummy smile to that
darling little boy looking back at you. It
was like you were asking him to be your
friend. I actually think that you already
understood that it was you that you saw.
        You also loved playing Peek-A-Boo.
Here, I was putting the blanket end of your
Doggie over your head and you would pull
it down and giggle at me when I said
"Peek-A-Boo, I see you" You were such a
happy baby and watching you discovering
the world around you was a thrill for us.
        I love you,
        Mom

7-21-2004

Paula's page is alive with energy due to the rhythm created by multiple square-cropped photos and lively patterns. She used a larger amount of patterned paper with a subtle design through the center of the page in order to not overpower the photographs. Likewise, bolder patterns were used in smaller quantities. Despite very different designs, the patterned papers contain all the same colors and thus coordinate perfectly. Journaling hidden behind the focal photo keeps the page clean.

Exploring 8 Months
Paula Barber, Allen, Texas

Supplies: *Patterned paper, frame, rub-on letters (KI Memories); textured cardstocks (Bazzill)*

Designer's eye

Simulate the ambiance of a place

Through detail photography of her wine glass, meal and buildings in Old Montreal, Christine captured the true ambiance of a quiet and relaxing winter afternoon. She shot without a flash to help capture the romantic old-world charm of the restaurant where they ate lunch. She printed all but one photo small to fit a lot of photos on the page and to create a symmetrical border along the top and bottom. Metallic accents complement the feel of the layout. Gray and rust cardstocks pick up the same colors found in her photos.

Old Montreal
Christine Stoneman, Cumberland, Ontario, Canada

Supplies: *Textured cardstocks (Bazzill); fleurs-de-lis metal charm (EK Success); decorative brads (Making Memories)*

So she'd never forget the excitement of moving into her new home, LeAnne made a spread highlighting her favorite features. She photographed each one and placed them side by side in a photo montage. A description of each feature is located below the photos in short columns. A mat of black cardstock backs all the photos to make them stand out from the background. A chipboard tile that Leanne designed herself balances the title on the opposite end.

My Favorite Things
LeAnne B. Fritts, Denver, North Carolina

Supplies: *Patterned paper (Chatterbox); letter stickers (American Crafts, Creative Imaginations); chalk ink (Clearsnap); cardstocks*

Mimic an advertisement

The color choices and color-blocked strip on Betsy's page were inspired by the television advertisements and Web site design for Pier 1 stores. The hues mesh well with her gray, green-eyed cat, and the "colors of you" concept allowed Betsy to document bits and pieces of her cat's personality. The light background in the photos contrasts well with the dark page background.

…You
Betsy Lombardi, Yonkers, New York

Supplies: *Image-editing software (Adobe Photoshop)*

Arrange photos on a diagonal line

A slightly diagonal line through this layout unifies the two sides and supports Lindsey's long-distance concept. Shots of her son were cropped at an angle and matted with cardstock to create a parallel line. The design was inspired by Bonnie Lotz.

Unlimited Long Distance
Lindsey Krauss, Monroe, New York

Supplies: Patterned papers (Junkitz); letter stickers, snap, mini brad (Making Memories); scrap metal (Remember When); word tag (Eyelet Outlet); transparency; circle clips; pen; cardstock

E

The little squirt of yours is getting to be quite a regular sight. You search the yard for bugs throughout the day and into the night.

Little bugs.

Big bugs.

Crawling bugs.

Flying bugs.

You find all the bugs on the ground and in the air. It's cute to watch you find them, but really, it's okay if you don't share.

THE

EXTERMINATOR

To unify this page, Linda silhouette-cut asterisk-type designs from a sheet of patterned paper. She placed them in three different areas to bring the layout together. Complementary colors of red and green make up the accents on her page, which draws from the photograph. She wrote a simple and whimsical poem to describe her son's love of bugs that fits perfectly with her playful subject.

The Exterminator
Linda Harrison, Sarasota, Florida

Supplies: *Patterned paper (Arctic Frog); textured cardstock (Bazzill); letter stickers (Chatterbox); letter tile (Making Memories); letter buttons (Junkitz)*

Complement design with the lines in a photo

Jennifer enlarged a photo of her daughter that displays her "art" all over their French doors. The clean lines of the door in the photo contribute to Jennifer's graphic style. A detail photo of the door and two others featuring her daughter with different expressions enhance the focal photo. She balanced the story of her daughter's little art project between a title and her daughter's name and age, both in the same bright shade of green.

So Busted!
Jennifer Perks, Round Rock, Texas

Supplies: *Cardstock*

Use contrasting type on a black background

Andrea reveals bits of her personality and celebrates womanhood on this simple layout inspired by her computer's screen saver. Plenty of open space around her title draws attention to it. One font style in different sizes fits with the simple, straightforward "I am" statements in her journaling.

All About Andrea
Andrea Victoria, Renton, Washington

Supplies: *Image-editing software (Adobe Photoshop 7.0); digital papers (Ooh La La Kit by Holly McCaig, www.thedigichic.com)*

Multiple photos of her son with expressions of laughter and smiles fit well with Kelly's page theme—her son telling his first joke. To add variation to the photos, Kelly inserted two cardstock squares on which she had printed the joke he told. Her title and journaling balance each other in the bottom section of the page. Soft pastel colors go with the lighthearted tone.

Joketelling 101
Kelly Goree, Shelbyville, Kentucky

Supplies: *Patterned paper (Autumn Leaves); textured cardstock (Bazzill); premade square accent (KI Memories); epoxy sticker (Making Memories)*

Mix horizontal and vertical elements

Christine's layout incorporates a mix of horizontal and vertical page elements. The focal photo spreads horizontally across the top of her page and is balanced with the vertically striped patterned paper below. Two pink and brown design elements with opposite orientations add to the simple, balanced look. With only one sentence of explanation, Christine captured the caring nature her husband has toward their children.

Sometimes
Christine Traversa, Joliet, Illinois

Supplies: *Patterned paper, letter stickers (Chatterbox); cardstocks*

Design elements can and should be repeated in a "visual triangle" to help complete a layout. In this page, color (light blue) and shape (circular) help round out the communication of the message.

Surround a strong focal point with fun elements

Kelly began her journaling with an initial capital letter that creates a striking design element. To balance the initial cap, she included a rub-on seal in the lower right corner. To allow photos of her boys to remain the focus of the page, she chose colorful patterned papers that have a muted quality. The papers coordinate with but do not overwhelm the bright blues and reds in the photos.

Drinking It In
Kelly Goree, Shelbyville, Kentucky

Supplies: *Patterned papers, rub-on elements (Basic Grey); textured cardstock (Bazzill); letter stickers (American Crafts); decorative scissors, corner rounder, circle punch (Creative Memories); pen; transparency*

Choose fitting page accents

A focal photo of a bored-looking subject, patterned paper consisting of random scribbles and a graphic image of a television come together to convey Deborah's son's feelings of summertime boredom. She recorded a conversion as an example of his situation. Deborah chose her title font because she thought it evoked the feeling of being trapped, which further enhanced her concept. The placement of type, images and title on her layout was inspired by an advertisement.

I'm Bored
Deborah Hodge, Durham, New Hampshire

Supplies: *Patterned papers (Imagination Project, Mara-Mi); textured cardstock (Bazzill); label maker (Dymo); page pebble (Making Memories); television dingbat (www.fontfreak.com)*

Unify a page with repeated colors

Lara recorded a darling conversation that captures her daughter's inquisitive nature and is sure to yield laughter from viewers of her album. The single-word title sums up Bria's most commonly used word. Title and journaling colors pull from the hues in her patterned paper, and colored brads in the top right corner unify the journaling block with the pattern.

Why
Lara Neves, Mesa, Arizona

Supplies: *Patterned paper (KI Memories); textured cardstocks (Bazzill); brads (Making Memories)*

Include a unique photo perspective

Time Out

A single photo of Tarri's son Jameson sitting alone behind a tree is actually a window into his personality. Jameson likes to go off and sit by himself whenever he can't do something well. As Tarri coined it, he likes to give himself a little time out. Her unique photo perspective captures one of those moments. She played off the red on her son's hat to accent the page along with black and white.

Time Out
Tarri Botwinski, Grand Rapids, Michigan

Supplies: *Patterned paper, tag, snap (Chatterbox); rub-on letters (Making Memories); ribbon (Offray); photo corners (3L); cardstock*

Riley, Jameson and Quinn were all out playing in the snow. They seemed to be having fun - making snowballs and rolling around. Then I spied Jameson walking away. He went and sat down behind the big maple tree in the front yard and tried hard not to let me see him.

I went over to find out what was wrong. He was upset about not being able to make a snow angel. When he can't do something well, he likes to go off by himself and think and try to get over what's bothering him. He gives himself a little time out.

Use photos with reflective qualities

These are more than detail shots of Christmas ornaments—in the reflection of the ornaments, one can see the artist. As a scrapbooker and not usually the main subject of her own pages, Ann wanted to portray herself through this perspective. The reflective nature of Ann's journaling regarding her love for scrapbooking also ties in to her concept. Digital textures along the top and bottom add symmetry to the page and coordinate with the colors and textures of her ornaments.

Digi Scrapper's Self Portrait
Ann Hetzel Gunkel, Chicago, Illinois

Supplies: *Image-editing software (Adobe Photoshop 7.0); scroll brush (April Anderton, www.digitalscrapbooking.com); digital patterned papers (Design Butcher's Architexts Collection, www.scrapgirls.com)*

Frame a photo with color blocking

A color-blocked background adds life to this page while still maintaining large open spaces. Like the description of her son, the layout appears quiet, yet colorful. The boy's portrait, with mouth closed, supports the "silent type" theme. A circular design element and initial in opposite corners balance the layout.

The Silent Type
Valerie Salmon, Carmel, Indiana

Supplies: *Textured cardstocks (Bazzill); label holder, mini brads (K & Company); circle cutter (Creative Memories)*

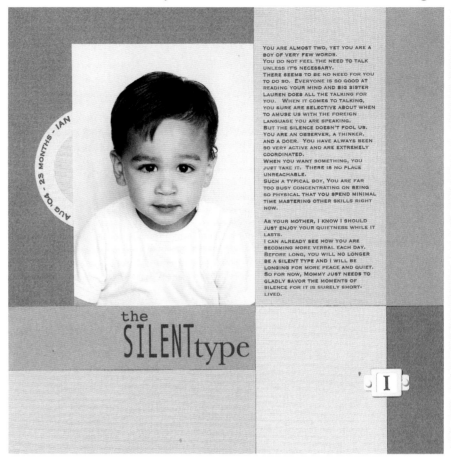

Pull page elements together with rounded corners

Emma's clean layout of black and gold cardstocks mimics the serene beauty of the sunset and a quiet evening out. Her photos all contain a similar warm glow, from the shot of the horizon to a detail shot of the meal. Rounded corners pull her photos, journaling and title together, creating one focal point that contains many smaller elements. She designed a tab with the place and date to mirror the shape of the larger main image. Emma designed the title using image-editing software, altering the letter "p" so the tail is extended.

Pintxos at Sunset
Emma Finlay, Sutton, Dublin, Ireland

Supplies: *Image-editing software (Adobe Photoshop 5.0); textured cardstocks (Bazzill); corner rounder (All Night Media)*

Unify a two-page spread with continuous lines

Debi has worked at the same job since 1991 and realized she'd never documented this very important part of her life. This spread is a tribute to her career and all the people she cares about. The diagonal line of photos adds rhythm to the layout and unifies the two pages by spanning across both. A title in the top left corner is balanced by a mini album in the bottom right corner. A single line of journaling beneath the photos draws viewers into them and adds detail. Other details are housed inside the mini album to keep the layout neat and clean.

You Call This Work?
Debi Boler, Newport Beach, California

Supplies: *Patterned paper (Chatterbox); ribbons (Making Memories); textured cardstocks, premade mini album (Bazzill)*

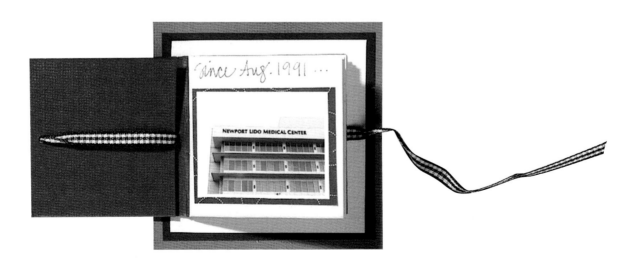

Design a symmetrical page

infr.v. **yakked**, also **yak**·**ing**, **yaks**,Prolonged, sometimes senseless talk; chatter.

"yakkers"

as John likes to call us. Whether Im sitting at the comp typing a novel or running away at the mouth on the phone, he knows it's one of two people and immediately shouts "yakkers" so they are aware he's now in the room. I don't think a day goes by that the three of us don't yak about one thing or another. In fact I don't think my day is complete without speaking to both of them. When one is feeling down, two of us are there to bring her up. We support each other no matter what, give advice whenever needed, and help wherever we can.

I'm not sure exactly when or how the 3 of became friends, in fact we have very different personalities, yet we mesh so well. Lindsey is the kindest most honest person I know and Wendy is so encouraging, always making sure I do my best and submit, submit, submit!! We have plans to meet one day, but for now I'm thankful to know them anyway I can. It's hard to believe that I can feel so close to two people I've never met, to know their kids, it's almost like they're mine too -geez that would make eight! I hope they know I love them and value their friendshio so much.

● Lindsey Bloom
lulubloom03

● Wendy Inman
saucywnch

● Teresa Olier
dragongoddess24

Teresa created a page as a tribute to her best long-distance friends, using their combined nickname as the title. Her layout is completely symmetrical: the page elements on one side are the exact mirror image of the other. A title spanning the width of the page, patterned paper strips on top and bottom, two columns of text and a horizontal row of photos all contribute to the symmetry. A wide gutter between the columns of text and wide leading between lines add to the clean, uniform feel.

Yakkers
Teresa Olier, Colorado Springs, Colorado

Supplies: _Patterned paper (Scrapworks); textured cardstock (Bazzill)_

Stack type to match a subject

To describe her favorite piece of furniture in her apartment, her bookshelf, Melissa placed her journaling and title in a stacked, bookshelf-like format. A tightly cropped photo of the shelf allows viewers to see many of the items on it that she describes. A small handstamped circle at the bottom is the only embellishment used.

My Space
Melissa Godin, Lorne, New Brunswick, Canada

Supplies: _Letter stamps (EK Success, FontWerks, PSX Design); circle punch (Fiskars); cardstock_

MY SPACE

ONE OF MY FAVORITE THINGS IN MY WHOLE APARTMENT IS MY BOOKSHELF. PAINTED MY FAVORITE COLOR (BROWN), IT SITS IN MY SCRAPBOOK ROOM WHERE IT HOLDS SOME OF MY FAVORITE THINGS. MY 'M' LETTER, MY ALTERED ITEMS, MY STORAGE BOXES AND BASKETS. I LOVE HAVING IT TO SHOWCASE MY LATEST AND GREATEST, BUT I LOVE JUST LOOKING AT IT. IT IS SO NICE AND TALL AND FULL OF INSPIRATION. I LOOK TO IT TO SEE WHAT I HAVE I MADE, AND TO SEE WHAT ELSE I CAN CREATE. IT'S A BIG HIT WITH VISITORS TOO. THEY LOVE TO SEE ALL MY GOODIES AND SOME HEAD STRAIGHT TO MY ROOM TO SEE WHAT IS NEW ON THE SHELF. MOST PEOPLE THAT WANDER TO THE BATHROOM CAN MOST TIMES BE FOUND IN FRONT OF THE BOOKSHELF. SOMETIMES IT CAN BE SO CROWDED, AND I HATE TO TAKE STUFF OFF OF IT. JAMIE KEEPS TELLING ME I NEED ANOTHER ONE, BUT THIS ONE IS SO PRETTY ALL BY ITSELF, WILL I EVER FIND ANOTHER JUST AS PERFECT!? I SUPPOSE I COULD ORDER OUT OF THE SAME CATALOGUE I GOT THIS ONE IN. TRUTH IS, I JUST WANT THIS ONE. STANDING TALL MAKING A STATEMENT, COOL & FUNKY— JUST LIKE ME.

Additional instructions & credits

Cover

You Are Priceless

Desiree designed her page around the concept of combining a well-known credit card company's hallmark word "priceless" with a price-scan barcode for a page title. She printed her barcode title directly onto cardstock, then framed the page in coordinating cardstock color blocks for unity. To help her photos stand out on a white background, Desiree added coordinating brads in a vertical arrangement that mirrors the lines of the barcode.

Desiree McClellan, Wichita, Kansas

Supplies: *Textured cardstocks (Bazzill, National); fonts (Price Check, www.twopeasinabucket.com); mini brads (Lasting Impressions)*

Page 1

Lexi

See instructions on page 103.

Page 3

If

The circle of patterned paper placed behind the matted photo helps draw attention to the short title, "If." Silver conchos with circular acrylic stickers inside them unify the patterned papers with the stark white background. The background also coordinates nicely with the black-and-white photo.

Karla Howard, McKinney, Texas

Supplies: *Patterned papers, conchos (Scrapworks); epoxy stickers (Colorbök); metal letters (Making Memories); cardstocks; stamping ink*

Page 8

I Love You

Monica had trouble getting a good shot of her daughter while playing at the water park, so she decided to explore another angle—literally! She used a photo of the backside of her daughter's bathing suit for the focal point. The layout features another clever twist in Monica's choice of words: "from the bottom of my heart."

Monica Schoenemann, Flower Mound, Texas

Supplies: *Patterned paper (NRN Designs); die-cut heart (Sizzix); ribbon, mini brads (Making Memories); cardstocks*

Page 36

I Don't Want To Grow Up

Desiree copied and pasted a line of text over and over to extend down her page, creating rhythm and the appearance of movement through repetition. She made some letters uppercase and changed the colors of different letters throughout for variation.

Desiree McClellan, Wichita, Kansas

Supplies: *Patterned paper, acrylic accent (KI Memories); cardstock*

Page 66

Je T' Aime Sens Dessus Dessous

See instructions on page 84.

Page 96

He's Getting Big

Julie created a balanced arrangement of photos, type and design elements in a page about her son. To play off the "getting big" theme, Julie enlarged the photo directly above the title, which in turn created a focal point. A tile with the first initial of her son's name successfully balances the bold title in the bottom right corner. Black matting around all photos help unify the page.

Julie Laakso, Howell, Michigan

Supplies: *Patterned paper (My Mind's Eye); textured cardstocks (Bazzill); letter stickers (Imagination Project); square brads, rub-on letters (Making Memories); chipboard letter (Li'l Davis Designs); label maker (Dymo)*

Cover	Page 3	Page 8	Page 36	Page 66	Page 96

   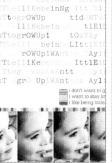  

Sources

3L Corp.
(800) 828-3130
www.scrapbook-adhesives.com

7 Gypsies
(877) 749-7797
www.sevengypsies.com

Adobe Systems Incorporated
(866) 766-2256
www.adobe.com

All My Memories
(888) 553-1998
www.allmymemories.com

All Night Media
(see Plaid Enterprises)

American Crafts
(801) 226-0747
www.americancrafts.com

American Traditional Designs®
(800) 448-6656
www.americantraditional.com

Arctic Frog
(479) 636-FROG
www.arcticfrog.com

Autumn Leaves
(800) 588-6707
www.autumnleaves.com

Basic Grey™
(801) 451-6006
www.basicgrey.com

Bazzill Basics Paper
(480) 558-8557
www.bazzillbasics.com

Berwick Offray, LLC
(800) 344-5533
www.offray.com

Bo-Bunny Press
(801) 771-4010
www.bobunny.com

Boxer Scrapbook Productions
(503) 625-0455
www.boxerscrapbooks.com

Broderbund Software
(319) 247-3325
www.broderbund.com

Canson®, Inc.
(800) 628-9283
www.canson-us.com

Chatterbox, Inc.
(208) 939-9133
www.chatterboxinc.com

Clearsnap, Inc.
(360) 293-6634
www.clearsnap.com

Close To My Heart®
(888) 655-6552
www.closetomyheart.com

Club Scrap™, Inc.
(888) 634-9100
www.clubscrap.com

Colorbök™, Inc.
(800) 366-4660
www.colorbok.com

Corel Corporation
(800) 772-6735
www.corel.com

Creative Imaginations
(800) 942-6487
www.cigift.com

Creative Inspirations—no contact info

Creative Memories®
(800) 468-9335
www.creativememories.com

Daisy D's Paper Company
(888) 601-8955
www.daisydspaper.com

Déjà Views
(800) 243-8419
www.dejaviews.com

Deluxe Designs
(480) 497-9005
www.deluxedesigns.com

Design Originals
(800) 877-0067
www.d-originals.com

Destination™ Scrapbook Designs
(866) 806-7826
www.destinationstickers.com

DieCuts with a View™
(877) 221-6107
www.dcwv.com

DMC Corp.
(973) 589-0606
www.dmc.com

Doodlebug Design™, Inc.
(801) 966-9952
www.doodlebug.ws

Dow Chemical Company, The
www.styrofoamcrafts.com

Duncan Enterprises
(800) 782-6748
www.duncan-enterprises.com

Dymo
(800) 426-7827
www.dymo.com

EK Success™, Ltd.
(800) 524-1349
www.eksuccess.com

Eyelet Outlet™
www.eyeletoutlet.com

Fibers by the Yard™
(405) 364-8066
www.fibersbytheyard.com

Fiskars®, Inc.
(800) 950-0203
www.fiskars.com

FontWerks
(604) 942-3105
www.fontwerks.com

Frances Meyer, Inc.®
(413) 584-5446
www.francesmeyer.com

Great Balls of Fiber
(303) 697-5942
www.greatballsoffiber.com

Happy Hammer, The
(303) 690-3883
www.thehappyhammer.com

Heidi Swapp/Advantus Corporation
(904) 482-0092
www.heidiswapp.com

Hero Arts® Rubber Stamps, Inc.
(800) 822-4376
www.heroarts.com

Imagination Project, Inc.
(513) 860-2711
www.imaginationproject.com

Jasc Software
(800) 622-2793
www.jasc.com

Jo-Ann Stores
(888) 739-4120
www.joann.com

JudiKins
(310) 515-1115
www.judikins.com

Junkitz™
(732) 792-1108
www.junkitz.com

K & Company
(888) 244-2083
www.kandcompany.com

Karen Foster Design
(801) 451-9779
www.karenfosterdesign.com

Lasting Impressions for Paper, Inc.
(801) 298-1979
www.lastingimpressions.com

Lazar Studiowerx, Inc.
(866) 478-9379
www.lazarstudiowerx.com

LazerLetterz
(281) 627-4227
www.lazerletterz.com

Li'l Davis Designs
(949) 838-0344
www.lildavisdesigns.com

Magic Scraps™
(972) 238-1838
www.magicscraps.com

Making Memories
(800) 286-5263
www.makingmemories.com

Mara-Mi, Inc.
(800) 627-2648
www.mara-mi.com

Marvy® Uchida/Uchida of America, Corp.
(800) 541-5877
www.uchida.com

Ma Vinci's Reliquary
http://crafts.dm.net/mall/reliquary/

Maya Road, LLC
(214) 488-3279
www.mayaroad.com

May Arts
(800) 442-3950
www.mayarts.com

me & my BiG ideas®
(949) 883-2065
www.meandmybigideas.com

Memory Creators
www.memorycreators.com

Michaels® Arts & Crafts
(800) 642-4235
www.michaels.com

Microsoft Corporation
www.microsoft.com

MoBe' Stamps!
(925) 443-2101
www.mobestamps.com

Mrs. Grossman's Paper
Company
(800) 429-4549
www.mrsgrossmans.com

Mustard Moon™
(408) 299-8542
www.mustardmoon.com

My Mind's Eye™, Inc.
(800) 665-5116
www.frame-ups.com

NRN Designs
(800) 421-6958
www.nrndesigns.com

Office Depot
www.officedepot.com

Paper Adventures®
(800) 525-3196
www.paperadventures.com

Perfect Ribbon Co.—no contact info

Plaid Enterprises, Inc.
(800) 842-4197
www.plaidonline.com

Prism™ Papers
(866) 902-1002
www.prismpapers.com

Provo Craft®
(888) 577-3545
www.provocraft.com

PSX Design™
(800) 782-6748
www.psxdesign.com

Punch Bunch, The
(254) 791-4209
www.thepunchbunch.com

Queen & Co.
(858) 485-5132
www.queenandcompany.com

QuicKutz, Inc.
(801) 765-1144
www.quickutz.com

Ranger Industries, Inc.
(800) 244-2211
www.rangerink.com

Remember When—no contact info

Rusty Pickle
(801) 746-1045
www.rustypickle.com

Savvy Stamps
(866) 44-SAVVY
www.savvystamps.com

Scenic Route Paper Co.
(801) 785-0761
www.scenicroutepaper.com

Scrappy Cat™, LLC
(440) 234-4850
www.scrappycatcreations.com

Scrapworks, LLC
(801) 363-1010
www.scrapworks.com

SEI, Inc.
(800) 333-3279
www.shopsei.com

Sizzix®
(866) 742-4447
www.sizzix.com

Stampin' Up!®
(800) 782-6787
www.stampinup.com

Sticker Studio™
(208) 322-2465
www.stickerstudio.com

Sweetwater
(800) 359-3094
www.sweetwaterscrapbook.com

Teeny Trims—no contact info

Treehouse Memories
(801) 318-6505
www.treehousememories.com

Tsukineko®, Inc.
(800) 769-6633
www.tsukineko.com

Wordsworth
(719) 282-3495
www.wordsworthstamps.com

Wrights® Ribbon Accents
(877) 597-4448
www.wrights.com

Index

A

Achromatic colors 76
Acronym 56
Additional Instructions & Credits 124
Advertisement-inspired 22, 27, 45, 52, 58, 60, 73, 81, 105, 113
Art-inspired 106
Asymmetry 107

B

Balance 63, 64, 77, 88, 99, 101-102, 108, 118

C

Cartoons 21-22
Childhood phrases/quotes 14-15, 17, 104, 119
Circular images 12, 39, 68-71, 73, 79, 84, 87, 89, 94-95, 106
Close-up photos 8, 14-15, 21, 23-24, 26, 34, 68-69, 75, 76, 81, 86, 101, 118-119
Comparisons 10, 11, 13, 24
Complementary colors 108, 115
Concept, Chapter 1 8-35
Contrast 12, 42, 44, 63, 64, 68, 75, 76, 116
Curved lines 73-74, 84, 87, 89, 92-93, 95
Curved type 39, 46, 59, 65, 71, 106

D

Designer's Eye 13, 18, 24, 31, 40, 46, 53, 58, 65, 70, 77, 82, 89, 94, 100, 107, 112, 118
Detail photos 16-18, 27, 32- 33, 71, 85, 103, 105, 109, 112, 120
Diagrams 23, 31
Different perspectives 17, 20-21, 28-29, 32-33, 120

H

Humor 15, 30, 33

I

Image, Chapter 3 66-95
Initial caps 20, 41, 46-47, 110, 118
Introduction 6

L

Layering type styles 40, 51, 55, 58, 116-117
Layout, Chapter 4 96-123
Line direction 77, 95, 108

M

Magazine-inspired 53
Movement/motion 35, 77, 84, 94, 95
Movie poster-inspired 29
Multiple fonts 38, 41, 51, 60-61

N

Newspaper-style 25

O

Open space 12, 18-19, 32-33, 38-41, 44, 64, 78, 88-89, 102, 109, 121

P

Passage of time 11-13
Patterns 68, 87, 88, 90, 91, 94
Photo manipulation 34, 80-84, 100, 104
Photo montage 28, 60, 85, 101, 103, 105, 111-113, 121
Play on words 8, 26, 27, 100
Primary colors 100

R

Repetition 11, 34, 36, 62, 68-69, 73, 84, 89, 98-99, 105, 109
Rhythm 36, 68-69, 73, 106, 109, 111

S

Secondary colors 104
Silhouette 82
Source Guide 125
Symmetry 27, 108, 120, 123

T

Table of Contents 4-5
Type, Chapter 2 36-65
Type overlaying photos 11, 15, 31, 43, 49, 51, 52, 54, 59, 74, 75, 78, 81, 105, 108

U

Unity 24, 68, 70, 84, 98, 100, 107, 114-115, 119, 122

V

Value (color) 103

W

Why It Works 10, 38, 68, 98

Learn more from these informative titles from Memory Makers Books!

Quick & Easy Scrapbook Pages
ISBN-13 978-1-892127-20-4
ISBN-10 1-892127-20-2
Paperback • 128 pgs. • #32471

Mastering Scrapbook Page Design With
Michele Gerbrandt
ISBN-13 978-1-892127-37-2
ISBN-10 1-892127-37-7
Paperback • 112 pgs. • #33005

Creative Scrapbooking With Your Computer
ISBN-13 978-1-892127-53-2
ISBN-10 1-892127-53-9
Paperback • 112 pgs. • #33359

More Quick & Easy Scrapbook Pages
ISBN-13 978-1-892127-56-3
ISBN-10 1-892127-56-3
Paperback • 128 pgs. • #33360

Creative Layout Variations
ISBN-13 978-1-892127-57-0
ISBN-10 1-892127-57-1
Paperback • 96 pgs. • #33362

Mastering Scrapbook Styles
ISBN-13 978-1-892127-55-6
ISBN-10 1-892127-55-5
Paperback • 128 pgs. • #33361

These books and other fine Memory Makers Books titles are available from your local art or craft retailer, bookstore or online supplier. Please see page 2 of this book for contact information for Canada, Australia, the U.K. and Europe.